D1080507

LIVERPOOL
COMMUNITY
COLLEGE

MOVES

ie for return on or be

6504200

Performing Arts Studies

A series of books edited by Christopher Bodman, London, UK

Volume 1
Music Unlimited
The Performer's Guide to New Audiences
Isabel Farrell and Kenton Mann

Volume 2
Experimental Music Notebooks
Leigh Landy

Volume 3
Inner Rhythm
Dance Training for the Deaf
Naomi Benari

Volume 4
Improvisation, Hypermedia and the Arts since 1945
Hazel Smith and Roger T. Dean

Volume 5
Moves
A Sourcebook of Ideas for Body Awareness and Creative Movement
Katya Bloom and Rosa Shreeves

Volume 6
Moving Notation
A Handbook for Musical Rhythm and Elementary Labanotation for the Dancer
Jill Beck and Joseph Reiser

In preparation
82 Scores
Paul Ramsay

MOVES

A SOURCEBOOK OF IDEAS
FOR BODY AWARENESS
AND CREATIVE MOVEMENT

Katya Bloom and Rosa Shreeves

harwood academic publishers

Australia • Canada • China • France • Germany • India
Japan • Luxembourg • Malayasia • The Netherlands • Russia
Singapore • Switzerland • Thailand • United Kingdom

Copyright © 1998 OPA (Overseas Publishers Association) Amsterdam B.V. Published in The Netherlands by Harwood Academic Publishers.

All rights reserved.

No part of this book may be reproduced or utilized in any form or by any means, electronic or mechanical, including photocopying and recording, or by any information storage or retrieval system, without permission in writing from the publisher. Printed in India.

Amsteldijk 166
1st Floor
1079 LH Amsterdam
The Netherlands

British Library Cataloguing in Publication Data

Bloom, Katya
   Moves: a sourcebook of ideas for body awareness and
   creative movement. – (Performing arts studies; v. 5)
   1. Movement (Acting)
   I. Title   II. Shreeves, Rosa
   792′.028

   ISBN 90-5702-133-1 (softcover)

Cover drawing by Rosa Shreeves

CONTENTS

Contents

PART THREE

INTRODUCTION TO THE SERIES

Performing Arts Studies aims to provide stimulating resource books of a both practical and philosophical nature for teachers and students of the performing arts: music, dance, theatre, film, radio, video, oral poetry, performance art, and multimedia forms.

International and multicultural in scope and content, *Performing Arts Studies* seeks to represent the best and most innovative contemporary directions in performing arts education, and will focus particularly on the work of practising artists who are also involved in teaching.

Christopher Bodman

LIST OF FIGURES

All figures drawn by Rosa Shreeves

ACKNOWLEDGEMENTS

We wish to thank all those who have inspired and enriched our work, our teachers, colleagues and students, from whom we have learned so much.

Our thanks go also to our editor Christopher Bodman for his support and creative suggestions.

PREFACE

Our collaboration began over ten years ago. At the time we were meeting to explore movement together and share ideas about the experience. We had both considered writing more about body awareness and creative movement and decided to pool ideas from our separate backgrounds and work on a book together. We explored and consolidated our ideas in both movement and writing, in so doing often generating new material.

In writing *Moves* we became fascinated by the actual process of writing with another and finding the best words to convey the movement experience. Writing, which is usually a very private process, took on a new dimension as we edited each other's work, sometimes combining pieces of our writing.

On the way we discovered links between our work and the ideas of other writers, artists and therapists. These connections are exemplified by the quotations interspersed throughout the text. The book was put together in a way similar to assembling a dance from various separate but interrelated motifs — a challenging and consistently rewarding process providing enrichment, both personal and professional.

INTRODUCTION

Moves is aimed at deepening awareness of the body and the self through the practice of movement and dance. We suggest a wealth of exercises which stem from the natural movement of the body, and are therefore accessible to anyone. Those who are disillusioned with a mechanical approach to exercise and are looking for something deeper which considers the body and the mind together will find this book a rich resource. It will be specifically useful for performers, educators and therapists.

The exercises in *Moves* take into consideration our physical, emotional and imaginative processes. Thus the book deals with both the internal experience of movement as well as its visible external form. The aim of *Moves* is to reawaken awareness of how the body *feels*, to rekindle the imagination and to provide starting points for developing both greater self awareness and expressive movement material.

Many people are familiar with feeling out of touch with their bodies and therefore out of touch with themselves. All too often we are "thinking heads", carrying our bodies around like suitcases, mostly unaware of them unless they break down. The intention here is to redress the balance. The following questions underline both the practical and theoretical nature of the book:

(1) Can movement be a means of integrating our mind, body and emotions?
(2) How can we learn more about ourselves through movement?
(3) How are we affected by our surroundings and the natural world?
(4) How can we use our bodies and therefore ourselves creatively?

This integrative approach to movement has been used with wide ranging groups of people of different ages and backgrounds, in schools and colleges, hospitals, within community settings and therapeutic situations, with dancers and actors, including those with special needs. The book is organized into three parts. Each part interweaves meditative awareness exercises with expressive movement. In general, there is a progression from:

1) initial focussing inward, and re-connecting to the self, to
2) developing the full use of the body through sequences of movement and improvisational frameworks, to
3) finding forms for fully embodying our emotions and connecting with the environment.

There is a natural progression from one group of exercises to the next, but in practice we encourage you to try finding your own logic with regard to what follows what. Play with the exercises according to how you feel. As adults we easily forget our need for play, and play is inherent to the creative process. So feel free to hop, skip and jump from exercise to exercise, section to section around the book as your curiosity and intuition suggest.

There is actually no prescribed outcome for any exercise. At any point during this work you may experience a moment when the 'movement' becomes 'dance', when all the parts of the experience — the body, the movement, the imagination, the use of space — come together. There is an intensity, a totality in the movement feeling which is not to do with expertise, but with complete immersion in and oneness with the movement. These times are almost impossible to put into words, but whether you are moving or watching movement, you inexplicably know when the 'dance' is there.

When leading a movement group, it goes without saying that you may well want to adapt the language and ideas to suit the people you are working with. When moving on your own, it can be helpful to tape record the text and then respond to it, especially some of the more meditative exercises. Gentle background music may be helpful on occasion to get you in the mood, but you may find the exercises so absorbing that they are fine without accompaniment.

Although some of the exercises define exactly what to do, others give stimulating images to which you can respond freely. The colourful language is used deliberately to enliven the imagination and elicit a fuller movement response. Similarly, informative passages have been interspersed with more poetic pieces of writing. The visual effect of different types of presentation might be compared to the changing rhythm and energy of movement itself. Reading about movement is not the same as experiencing it, but this book aims to make a bridge between words and sensation.

In practising these exercises you are practising a process, a way of deepening your connection to yourself as well as acquiring movement skills. The movement and self-awareness develop alongside each other. Noticing what you want and need to do, from one moment to the next, is in itself a skill, perhaps the most important skill of all. Feel free to repeat movements many times in order to find out more, not only about the specifics of an exercise, but also about the underlying principles which can gradually be absorbed. Be gentle with yourself. Strain is not conducive to the process, so take care to adapt the material to what feels right for you. As you respond to the material in *Moves*, you may notice changes in yourself. You may feel a greater physical and emotional freedom, a lessening of anxiety and constriction. You may experience a new found sense of flow, flexibility and strength, greater responsiveness to others and to the environment, sharper intuition, and an increased sense of choice and possibility so that you feel more fully functioning and alive.

PART ONE

1

INNER LOOKING AND LISTENING

Through our physical selves we receive sensory information and impressions from the outside world. We interact with our surroundings by means of our senses, our movement and our responses. We experience ourselves through our bodies. Within ourselves we make sense of the external world and at the same time use our thoughts and imaginings to propel courses of action. Our inner world of feelings, dreams, memories and images is as real and necessary to us as food and water. When we nourish both our unique inner world and our interaction with the outer we may find a balance, a state of being which is neither too inturned nor over active. In a receptive state energy from ourselves can flow outwards and energy from without can flow in. We are connected to all life.

It is when we are still and silent that we can most easily contact our inner world and connect it to our outer experience. To observe yourself in stillness is a meditative discipline, to gradually bring the body and mind to rest so that you finally arrive at the place of stillness...and you settle into that place for as long as you like. In the beginning of tuning in to the world of inner space, the flow of feelings, the sensations of bones and muscles, there is a waiting period, a transition time for calming and slowing, leaving the outer world of thinking and doing behind and receiving the impressions of your inner world.

Inner listening is a quiet, attentive tuning in, with a willingness to accept all that is in you, and a curiosity to discover all that you are. Stillness is the place to begin from, to go consciously out to the moving, thinking and doing of life. There is a rhythmic flow for all of us between movement and stillness. We can grow to consciously know and respond to this pattern.

Emptying

> Opening the pores of the skin...
> Loosening the tissues of the

muscles and the organs
Quietening the chatter of the mind...
Emptying the body of excess tension
What remains is the quiet flow of breath
the pulsing of heart and blood
and the warm secure knowledge that
YOU are there...deeply permeating your every cell
with the Essence that is you.

Basic positions

Throughout the book the basic body positions of

folded position
sitting
standing
kneeling on all fours
or, lying down on the back

are frequently suggested as starting positions.

Before beginning any exercise, take some time to become aware of yourself in the starting position. Feel your contact with the ground. Try to release any unnecessary tension in your body. Aim for a balanced position where the right and left sides of your body are equal. Think of your head as in line with your spine, not pulled back or thrusting forward or off to one side. Often we have habitual imbalances in our posture but generally these become less as our body awareness increases.

Folded position

Sitting back on your heels, forehead resting on the floor. Notice the placement of the different parts of your body in the starting positions to help you get the most out of each exercise.

Sitting

Legs crossed or soles of the feet touching. Back straight but relaxed. Shoulders and arms hang down easily.

Standing

Head in line with the spine. Feet straight forward a little apart. Think of the base of the spine dropping as the arms hang, the knees soften and the head floats up. This helps avoid a rigid back, and allows its natural curves.

Kneeling on all fours

Hands under shoulders. Knees under hips. Spine relaxed and outstretched.

Moves

Lying down on your back (a)

Head centred in line with your spine. Arms relaxed outstretched or at your sides. Legs flopped outwards and the back of the neck long.

Or:

Lying down on your back (b)

Knees bent, feet flat on the floor. Knees and feet a little apart. Find the most comfortable, balanced position for your legs and back.

"At the beginning of a movement session I am more aware of my surroundings than myself. I have no interest in my body. I do not feel. The idea of moving is remote. I listen to the traffic. I notice the chilly room. In other words I focus on my surroundings, allowing them to distract me from myself. I need to 'listen' inwards".

A sitting meditation

Use this exercise for focussing inwards, leaving behind all concerns and distractions. Find an easy balanced sitting position, against a wall or on a cushion perhaps. Close your eyes to begin

Sit on the floor
Motionless as a stone
Listen in the stillness
To the sounds around you

Then like focussing a camera
Clearly "see" the whole shape of you
A cut out in stillness
Visualise yourself sitting ...
The position you are in
Your contact with the floor
The placement of your hands
The angle of your head
Your ... spine ... line

Then slowly zoom in through
Your outer self into your interior
Feel the movement of breath
Direct it towards your centre
Let it warm your interior
Like a radiator

Inner warmth and outer shape
Connect them through your breath
Then open your eyes and
Return to your surroundings.

Visualization

We all have the ability to visualize, to create mind pictures or mental images. One of the most important ways we have of bringing the mind and body together is through the use of visualization. In movement we visualize or "see" an image in our mind and at the same time, we allow our body to absorb the image and respond to it. The image may be directed to the body as a whole or towards a specific body part. The use of visualization is exemplified in many of the exercises throughout the book.

There was a startling change in the quality of experience itself when imagination was brought down to earth and made incarnate in the body.

Marion Milner
On Not Being Able to Paint

Breathing meditations

The following four exercises use different images to increase awareness and sensitivity, and produce subtly different responses in the body. One exercise or even a small part of one may hold your attention for a long time. Use breathing, particularly the outbreath, to soften and release the muscles and the mind. Breathe with ease, not effort.

Watching your breath

Lie down in a quiet place. Stretch out and sink down.
With eyes closed, begin to focus on your breath,

Without controlling it, changing it
or judging it. Just watch it.
Where in your body do you feel your breath to be?
Rest your hands on top of that place.
As your hands feel the place from the outside,
Use your mind's eye to
See the place on the inside.

Notice the movement of your breath
The inhale ... and the exhale ...
Be aware of the space in time
Between the end of one breath and the
Beginning of another. Do not hurry.
Allow the breath to breathe you.

Letting go

As you practice lying still and turning your attention inside your body, see
whether you can observe the subtle ways in which you hold yourself UP and
hold yourself TOGETHER by habitual but unnecessary tightening of muscles.
       What would happen if you let go of EVERYTHING and let the floor
have the full weight of your body?

Lying down on your back
Be aware of your breathing ...
Of stillness ...
Feel the contact of your body
With the ground
Notice all the parts in contact
Let the ground support you
So you do not need to
Hold on to any part of you.

Let go in the hip joints
So the legs relax outwards
From the hip sockets
Let go in the shoulder joints
So the arms relax ...
Feel the weight of the head
Imagine the front of your body
Opening and softening

Breathe gently. Feel you exhale
Through your back and
Into the floor as though you
Sink below the
Surface of the floor

Let the exhale last a
Long time. Follow it
D
-
O
-
W
-
N

"I felt so peaceful. It really gave me time to be with myself, just to be quiet. I think that's really important."

— An eighty year old woman who experienced
this exercise in her wheelchair

Directing your breath

To increase your awareness and sensation in any particular area of your body, aim your breath right into that part. Directing the breath opens up a channel of awareness, a consciousness of that part.

Before you direct your breathing into a place, your MIND is already there. The body part already feels itself.

Thoughts for directing your breath

Breathe down into your stomach and pelvis. Visualize the diaphragm moving down as you breathe in.

Inhale and imagine breath going into your hip joints or touching and loosening any stiff parts of yourself.

Breathe up into your head filling it like a balloon.
Breathe right down to the soles of your feet.

Dissolving restrictions

As you grow accustomed to sensing and feeling the inner spaces and places of your body, you may begin to notice areas that seem 'dark' or 'dead' or 'missing'. At present they may seem to lie just below the realm of consciousness. Simply notice these places. They are the "black holes" of your body awareness. In time, by giving these places your attention, the dark areas gradually become more illuminated.

> Focus on your breathing and
> Imagine the breath filling
> Your body like a
> White light
> Channelling through
> Dissolving away restrictions.
> See your breath
> Lighting up the whole region inside.
> Imagine the tissues illumined by the breath.
> Breath like waves, advancing and retreating.
>
> On the exhale imagine that you
> Breathe out any tensions or
> Unwanted thoughts
> Breathe away the rubbish
> Inhale energy and life.

As you explore these ideas, notice any changes that may occur in your breathing, your body awareness or your state of mind, and any images that may surface.

> *So open wide the whole body.*
> *Receive the incoming tide of space*
> *Open the body from the centre.*
> *So that your whole being can absorb*
> *all that wishes to be felt and known by you.*

Raden Ayou Jodjana
A Book of Self Re-Education

The inner volume

> As you lie quietly breathing
> Let your mind go down beneath the surface of your skin.

In your mind's eye, scan this inside space . . .
Imagine your head hollow like a balloon,
Observe the tube of your neck,
Feel the width across your shoulders,
Then, take a slow journey along your spine,
From the base of your skull all the way to your tailbone.

Notice the width of your torso and
The depth from front to back.
Travel the length of your arms,
And the long, long length of your legs.
Feel your entire body underneath the surface of your skin.
Fill it with your breath.

The aerial view

Imagine taking an aerial view of your body
As you lie stretched out on the floor.
See your whole shape from the top of your head
To the soles of your feet.
Feel yourself from the inside as you
See yourself from the outside.

"I feel I can fill out my body now. I'm not just a head."
— A drama student

Fifteen minutes to stand up

Try taking a long, long time to get from lying down to standing . . .

Start lying on your back on the floor.
Know that you have fifteen minutes to get to standing
and you won't arrive early.
Simply listen to your body to find out which part
feels like moving first.
Slowly begin to stretch
Like waking up from a deep sleep . . .
moving as you wish, being still when you like
Savour each movement you make
on this slow journey from horizontal to vertical.

Explore all the levels, shapes, thoughts and positions
along the way.
It's a timeless dance of inner listening.

This exercise could help you make a transition from a still meditative state
into movement.

She seemed hardly to move. It wasn't a group of gestures or a fixed pattern of steps.
It had little to do with dance and yet it was the essence of all great dancing ... to
convey a feeling, to make a suggestion and when it was done, we were different.

Lyall Watson
Gifts of Unknown Things

Standing meditation

Stand with your feet hips-width apart
Close your eyes and focus inside yourself.
First notice the contact of your feet
With the ground. Feel the ground
Beneath your toes, the balls of your feet
And your heels.
Imagine your kneecaps softening and
Letting go.
Sway a little.
Feel gently balanced on your feet.

Focus now on your spine
Imagine what it looks like
Let your thoughts climb slowly up the
Vertebrae to where the head balances on
The atlas bone at the top. Feel your
Shoulders hang like a yoke.
Let your head float upwards, lengthening you.

Feet on the ground, head high
You make a connection between
Earth and sky.
Draw earth energy up and sky energy down
Let them intermingle.
Breathe out through your
Heels into the ground.

> Experience your unique self,
> Standing.

Moving with awareness

All the experience that we have of ourselves is by way of our bodies and through our movement. To move with awareness we need to focus on how we are feeling now, in this present moment. By constantly looking ahead or glancing behind we may lose the experience of the present.

Moving with awareness entails paying attention to the physical details of our movement. We are usually unaware of these in our everyday activities. Our thoughts are focussed on the external activity rather than on the internal feel of the movement and the nuances within it.

Initially to move with awareness demands that you move slowly so that you have time to be aware of details. Through slow movements the mind begins to tune into the body. In the process the mind may become calmer and more focussed. The mind and body integrate into a common pace. The energies of the two begin to harmonize.

Meditative walking in a circle

Use simple repetition to develop awareness of this most basic of movements within the age old, ritualistic pattern of the circle.

> Walking in a circle
> Thinking into the feet
> Feeling the ground beneath
> Notice the gentle repetition of
> Your foot contact, follow
> The pulse of your movement . . .
> Walking on and on
> Feeling the energy begin to build
> Above the ongoing rhythm of your feet.
>
> Let your upper body and arms
> Start to move and dance
> circling twisting stretching breathing
> The whole of you carried along
> In the meditative calm
> Of the constant circle.

SUMMARY — INNER LOOKING AND LISTENING

This section has offered you ways of beginning to switch gears from thinking into feeling, to take a breath and to bring your attention down into your body. The emphasis has been on a slow, meditative approach, staying with the present moment and simply experiencing that, first of all in stillness and then gradually to moving with awareness into standing and walking. We have looked at a variety of ways to begin to focus inward, through

> – awareness of the body in different positions
> – watching the breath
> – relaxation and letting go

Slowly, slowly, by working in this way, we begin to connect the various aspects of ourselves, the mental, the physical and the emotional.

> *"...we need to integrate the body, breath and mind.*
> *When we learn to relax the body, breath and mind,*
> *the body becomes healthy, the mind becomes clear*
> *and our awareness becomes balanced."*

> Tarthang Tulku
> *Gesture of Balance*

This process is taken further in the next section with the use of touch and physical contact.

2

GETTING IN TOUCH

Throughout our lives we use the touch of our hands to comfort ourselves, to hold ourselves when afraid or cold — to rub hurt places and to protect ourselves. Perhaps unconsciously we connect to physical memories even in the womb when we were constantly "in touch" with our surroundings. We need the experience of human touch to nourish and strengthen our sense of self.

Self massage

Through self massage we can soften, lengthen, release and energise all the parts of our bodies that feel drab, sore and immovable. We can affect the muscles, nerves, organs and circulation towards a greater sense of self-awareness and well-being. From this experience we can learn what feels good to us and use this information in both self-healing and the use of touch with others.

Use the following ideas freely as a guide. Your body will suggest to you where it needs attention. Contrast more active phrases with meditative stillness, and try closing your eyes sometimes.

Massaging the whole body — A soothing once-over

Begin by sitting comfortably on the floor — use a cushion if necessary and find a position in which you can sit in stillness without strain. Then centre yourself, focussing your thoughts inward towards the centre of your body. Place your hands gently on your lower abdomen. This area just below your navel, your centre of gravity, is an important energy centre in the body. Feel the warmth of your hands and breathe there.

> Then without losing contact
> Smooth down the thighs, legs and feet
> Find your way
> Over your back and front
> Around your hips, neck and face and

> Try firm stroking all over
> Your arms and shoulders.

Take time slowly smoothing and stroking firmly along the surfaces of your body with your hands. In this way bring all the parts of your body into awareness.

Massaging body parts

When you feel looser and warmer try massaging specific parts of your body in turn. Just to massage one body part can be very satisfying and can have an effect upon the whole body.

Legs and hips

With your hands, smooth and squeeze up your leg muscles, kneading the calves, thighs and hips. Think of loosening and lifting the muscle off the bone. Press in around the joints. Then stroke up and down your legs with a long continuous stroke. Make a warming circle on the base of your spine with your whole hand. Then with your fists, gently pound all over your buttocks. This helps wake up your brain!

Hands and arms

Work on one hand at a time. Squeeze the wrist, palm and fingers. Soothe and stroke them. Press into the hand front and back, feeling the bones and the soft places between them. Smooth down and up each arm tracing the shape. Then, holding your wrist, wiggle and wave your passive hand, loosening wrist and fingers.

Skull

Place your hands on your head. Then, pressing down with your palms, move your skin gently over your scalp keeping your hands as relaxed as possible. Now use your fingertips to press down firmly into all the different parts of the skull, working into tender spots especially at the base of the skull.

Finally, as if brushing your hair back, use long luxurious strokes up over the forehead, over the skull, down the back of the neck and along and off the shoulders.

(See pages 84–87 and 129 for additional self massage ideas.)

"I had this strange experience on the way home after the class. I looked around me at the people on the tube and I felt as if I was seeing them not just with my eyes but with my whole body."

— A twenty-six year old business man

Rolling

Through physical contact with the floor we can re-establish a sense of our own reality. By literally 'coming down to earth' we can ground ourselves.

Try this exercise with your eyes closed.

Curling foetus-like, soft and rounded
Gently begin to roll.
Make a rolling journey
Across the floor
Travel over hip, pelvis
Lower back, shoulder, knee and thigh
Feel the gentle contact of
All your body surfaces
With the ground
Roll yourself out of your
Habitual shapes and directions
Roll into new territory.

Floor duet — contacting your bones

This exercise is designed to help you feel all the bones in your body by feeling them in contact with the floor.

Begin by settling into a relaxed position on the floor,
Notice where your body makes contact.
Take as long as you need, working very methodically,
to meet the floor with every part of your skeleton.
Use the floor to press against, or
sink into your bones.
Think of it as a massage.
Use your ribcage, pelvis, skull, even the sides
of your body.
Don't leave out the hard to get at areas.

Observe the strange shapes you find yourself in
along the way.
Go slowly, focussing on the bones.

A slow weighty journey

We need to keep a balance between the relaxation needed for ease in everyday movement and the appropriate amount of tension to support the body. There is a subtle balance between giving way to body weight — relaxing — and using it to move — pressing away from the floor. Note the feelings associated with these contrasting experiences.

From lying on your back.
Slowly roll over onto your side
Curling as you go
Breathe down through your weight
Giving way to gravity.

Then using your hands
Push yourself
Slowly to half sitting
Feel yourself pour downwards.

Now continue to move through
Different positions — sitting, kneeling
Lying, crawling, pressing away from the floor or
Softening into it, pausing on any part
of your body.

Each time feel where your weight is supported
Embody the shapes you discover
And finally slide down
To rest on the floor again.

Combining movements

There is something very pleasing about combining movements into a sequence, becoming familiar with the rhythmic and spacial implications of the phrase and allowing your perception of the movements to deepen with each repetition. It is like following the melody of a song. The following exercise exemplifies this.

A certain pathway

Use this exercise to bring greater awareness to different parts of the body through contact with the ground and through feeling your weight in each position.

> Stand with your feet parallel and a little apart.
> Breathe deeply and exhale slowly
> Down into your feet and
> Through the soles of your feet
> Into the ground.

> Slowly let your head hang down forwards
> And let it pull your head and upper body
> Downwards towards the floor.
> Hang down ... exhale.

> Bend your knees and gently walk your hands
> Forward along the floor until you rest on
> Hands and knees, head and belly
> Relaxed.

> Fold back onto your heels, arms stretched in front
> And roll over like a
> Seal onto your back
> Head relaxed, knees to your chest.

> Then roll on across your shoulder blades
> And pelvis until you kneel once more.
> Take time to stand very slowly, head up last.
> Walk a few paces and then
> Stand, kneel, fold and roll again ...

Find your own variations on the theme of standing, kneeling, folding and rolling. Can you find any underlying significance in this phrase, perhaps a journey backwards to childhood or a connection to evolutionary stages in movement?

I have come to feel that the only learning which significantly influences behaviour is self discovered, self appropriated learning. Such self discovered learning, truth that has been personally appropriated and assimilated in experience, cannot be directly communicated to another.

Carl Rogers
On Becoming a Person

See yourself move

> Try becoming more aware
> Of what a movement looks like
> As well as what it feels like
> As you move try visualizing yourself moving
> Like running an internal film of your action.
>
> Also, in stillness, use visualization
> To prepare you to move
> Try running through a movement in your head
> Before you do it
> Practise and remember movements internally.
>
> Then add a running commentary to your process —
> Describe in words what you are doing or feeling
> As you visualize and move . . .

Resting places

Use the following specific body positions for simply resting in stillness. Let go of tensions as you exhale deeply, releasing your weight, softening your joints and lengthening your spine. Just allow yourself to rest in each position. Feel it soften and deepen the longer you stay. Choose from the following resting positions:

1. Lying on your back, with legs stretched out or knees bent and feet flat on the floor.
2. Lying on your back, knees to your chest, holding your knees with clasped fingers.
3. The folded position, sitting back on your heels, forehead resting on the floor.
4. Wide-legged squatting, with head relaxed forward and heels on or off the floor.
5. Sitting cross-legged, back against the wall.
6. Lying on your back with your feet on the wall, legs straight or slightly bent.
7. Lying stretched out on your front.

> Let your thoughts slow down, thin out, float away.
> Let your energy gradually settle.

Know you are here, now, in this moment.
Feel this calm, still place,
Where your flow of breath merges with your peace of mind.

Finding your own resting places

Now find your own ways into and out of the suggested places, as well as
finding your own body shapes for resting in.
Feel these shapes like pieces of sculpture.

Fill the shape with your breath and stay in each shape until you feel an impulse to move on.

As you move through different body positions the gravitational pull on your
body changes. You will experience your own weight differently, e.g. notice
the different sense of weight in lying down to being on all fours.

Play with experiencing unusual positions — the tendency is to be less aware
in familiar or habitual positions.

"Especially in stillness I can really notice how I tighten my neck. That's my pattern."

— A young woman in a movement class

SUMMARY — GETTING IN TOUCH

In this section the emphasis has been on deepening the connection to the
body by experiencing its weight, by feeling the skin and bone and muscle,
and experiencing the effect of gravity. We focus deeply on GROUND-
ING ourselves through

> self massage and
> moving in contact with the floor

When we can literally feel that we are "inside our own skin", we begin
to know what it is to be grounded, to really be present. As a result of
these exercises we may feel calmer and more relaxed.

*"I had begun to guess that my greatest need might be to let go and be free from the
drive after achievement . . . I might be free to become aware of some other purpose
that was more fundamental . . . which grew out of the essence of one's own nature."*

Marion Milner
A Life of One's Own

In letting go of unnecessary tension, we have more available energy.

3

CONNECTING TO YOUR ENERGY

Up to this point in the book, the emphasis has been on beginning with slow, meditative movement to bring the mind and body together, to synchronize them. However it is possible to begin more actively and then gradually to slow down and tune inwards. Or try mixing and alternating between active and meditative states depending upon your intuitive rhythmic sense and needs of the moment.

The following exercises provide opportunities to explore this more energetic way of beginning.

"Sometimes I come to a session so tired I don't see how I can move at all, but I'm always surprised at how much energy I get from moving."

Shaking

Begin in the hands, shaking fingers lightly, thinking bones.
Feel the shaking grow from the wrist joint . . .
into the elbow . . . and the shoulder, till the whole arm
releases and loosens.
Pick up this movement in your head and upper spine as they
join in the skeletal shaking.

Begin again with a foot. Shaking from the ankle,
then the knee, then the hip,
try to shake your leg off.
One leg then the other.
Shake your pelvis. See the pelvis as your shaking centre
and feel the movement ripple through your whole body.

Swinging

Begin with one arm swinging.
Enjoy the rhythm, the momentum, the arc through space.

Experience the swing fully as you can, the drop and lift,
Swing out your breath and catch it on the suspend.
Let the swing build in speed and depth as you go.
Experiment with swinging two arms.

Now slowing to stillness,
Find the curved swing of your head side to side.
Let the swing grow
To include more and more of your spine.

Try leg swings; they will challenge your balance on one leg.
Then full body swings forward and back, side to side,
swinging in any direction.

Play with the theme of swinging.
Let the swinging take you for a ride
jumping, flying, travelling.

"I'm running! I'm running! I'm getting my energy! I'm getting my energy! I'm running!"

— A three year old girl

Twisting

From standing
Twist the upper body around
How far can you see
Behind you?
Use the joints in the arms
Then the legs, to explore
Twisting.

Through twisting we can
See so much more
Twisting can take you into
Turning, falling, rolling, spiralling
with an ever changing
Focus.

Bouncing

Begin the bouncing movement in your knees and ankles.
Imagine a rubber ball on the base of your spine

Bouncing you up and down
Bounce your shoulders loosely
Then the top of your head into the space above you
Let your arms swing and flop
As if they are attached by strings
To your shoulder sockets.

Have soft bouncing feet with
Toes not leaving the floor, then
Jumping higher.
Enjoy every part of you bouncing.

Feel the rhythm
Bounce with the rhythm of the earth
Bounce the world around with your feet.

Let the bouncing die down to stillness
Feel your feet connecting to the ground
Listen to your breathing.
Blow out your breath.

Listen to your heartbeat. Feel the
Blood coursing through your veins
Become still in the stillness around you
Standing, alive and full of energy.

Bouncing

Tapping and Patting

Use the tapping and patting to wake up your whole body, to refresh your body and your mind.

Start at the top of your head, using a quick and firm tapping motion of your fingertips. Tap all over your scalp. Move on to your face with quick and delicate pats. Continue these under your chin and down around your neck. Increase the pressure of patting as you move across the back of your shoulders, around to your chest and up and down your arms.

Continue to find your own rhythm of tapping and patting, covering your whole body . . . ribs, hips, legs, feet. Don't forget your back.

Measure the force and speed of your tapping to meet the different body surfaces. Taps may turn to easy slaps or punches around the hips and thighs.

Analysis of a yawn

Yawning is usually a spontaneous action, and we can be 'infected' by some-one else's yawn. We can also make ourselves yawn.

Try going through the motions of yawning, until you find yourself yawning for real.

To yawn:

First you have to open your mouth very wide
Then you take a sort of gasping breath in,
opening the back of your throat.
Then you release the breath out and close your mouth.
Your eyes may water, your nose run or you may swallow.

After just a few yawns you should feel heavier, more relaxed, and wonderfully into your body through a deep merging with your breath.

Take repeated yawns before you begin moving, and let the yawns lead you naturally into stretching.

SUMMARY — CONNECTING TO YOUR ENERGY

The exercises in this section have offered you many alternatives for an energizing body wake up through emphasizing

    – full participation of the whole body
    – letting movements grow and change and
    – enjoying the rhythm and flow of movement

Sometimes we feel the need for vigorous movement even at the begin-ning of a movement session. It all depends on how we feel. Slowing down, speeding up, using large or small movements... One thing we can be sure of, our condition will always change.

"Spend your power lavishly; it is inexhaustible, and the more you give, the more it will accumulate."

Michael Chekov
To the Actor

PART TWO

4

LENGTHENING AND LOOSENING

In this section continue exploring how you can deepen your sensitivity to your body through movement. Bring the concentration of your mind and the attention to your breathing into the easy lengthening and loosening movements in this section. Use these gentle stretching exercises for toning muscles to support the bones, for letting go of excess tension, and for creating space for yourself both physically and emotionally.

As you work in this way, lengthening and loosening, your perception may change as your whole body opens to your experience. Although contraction, closing into yourself, might feel more familiar and safer, try expanding as a way of becoming more alive, stronger. Through the sensual, yawning sensation of these exercises, you may feel a little more at home within yourself.

Breathing stretches

The more you integrate your breathing with the rhythm and flow of your movement, the more involved you may become.

> From any starting position
> Inhale as you stretch away
> from your centre
> into the space around you — opening yourself
> using any parts of your body, then
> Exhale and soften back into a
> different body shape.

> Try the opposite
> Exhale into your stretch
> Imagine breathing out through
> your body into the space.

> Breath becomes multi-directional energy
> as you play with breathing

and stretching, your whole self
Pulsing with energy.

As you contact your power in this exercise you may find yourself making energetic vocal sounds too — breath leading to sound, strengthening both the physical and emotional quality of the movement.

Tension release

Where there is tension or stiffness in the body there will be less physical sensation. We actually feel less in those parts of our bodies. If we can release excessive muscular tension we increase our sensitivity and consequently can move with greater ease and subtlety of expression.

Movement becomes more pleasurable as our awareness of it increases. Through this inner observation we become familiar with the feelings of our bodies. This awareness also makes us less accident-prone as we listen to ourselves more.

Wake up stretches

Use the idea of lengthening any two body parts
away from each other . . . preferably as you y-a-w-n . . .
For example,
Lengthen your legs away from your arms.

Think of a rubberband being stretched in two directions
at once.

Or the right leg away from the left arm in a long diagonal
stretch...

Or twist a shoulder away from a hip...an elbow from a knee...
Feel the countertension pull you in two directions.
Find your own favourite wake up stretches.

You might choose two body parts that feel less aware or alive
and begin to connect them through movement.

Seaweed spine

"Dance is aquatic, and the dancers are the fish."

George Balanchine.

> Imagine lying on the sea bed
> Freely ripple through your spine,
> From tail to head and head to tail.
> From the middle to both ends.
> Opening and closing
> Between the joints of the spine
> Twisting, spiralling
> Freely flowing like seaweed
> Underwater
> Breathe out like blowing bubbles
> Weightless, disorientated, ongoing
> Arms and legs are tendrils
> Dragged through currents
> Generated by the spine.

Try this exercise from standing too; a sea plant perhaps, rippling through the
imaginary sea.

Starfish stretch

Lie on your back starfish shape
Relax, feel yourself sink into the floor
Then
From the centre of your body
Imagine currents of energy streaming outwards
Along both arms and legs, your neck and head
Lengthening you out into
Five directions at once . . .
A star fish stretch as you inhale.

Breathe out as you
Roll from your back
To curl up on your side.
Imagine the top of your head
Curving forwards towards the base of
Your spine
Rest there.

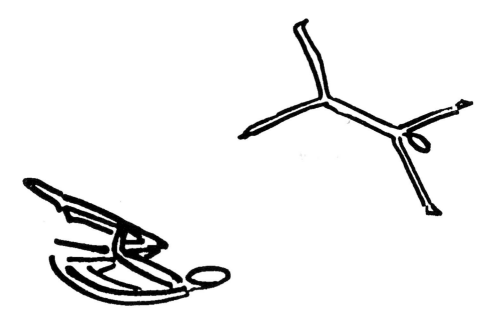

Continue this pattern of starfish lengthening and curling from one side of the body to the other, as you inhale and exhale. Then, if you like, allow the image to move you where it will.

Inner intention

Each exercise emphasizes a particular movement idea, for example, lengthening . . . a specific body part . . . the spatial direction etc. The focus initially is on that particular idea. Then as we move and deepen the experience of the exercise other awarenesses may come in as we relate personally to the content, e.g., noticing a tight part of the body, or a particular pattern of breathing or a sudden image arising.

The focus may change. There may be awareness on several different levels. So the exercise may be thought of as a source of information rather than an end in itself. It is the individual's personal awareness of the movement experience that is important.

Escalator spine

For lengthening the spine and increasing awareness of the joints.
From lying on your back — knees bent — feet flat on the floor

Feel your spine in contact
With the floor. Imagine
Each bone resting there
Picture your spine
LENGTHENING.

Slowly, supporting yourself through
Your feet and shoulders
Lift the base of your spine
Skywards, arching up . . .
Breathe down through your shoulders.

Then gradually let the spine return
To the floor smoothly descending
Down from the shoulders
To the sacrum
Bone by bone like an
Escalator.

Arm cycle

Through isolating the movement of the arms you can focus both on their lengthening and on their connection to the long muscles either side of the spine.

Lie on your back, knees up, arms at your sides
Then slowly stretch and lift your arms
Up and over to rest on the floor
Above the head
Feel the stretch there
Keep your back in contact with the floor
And your neck long
Rest there for a moment
And then lengthen the arms over and
Back down to your sides again.

Connect this movement to long sighing exhales. Notice the weight of the arms. Feel the connection between your fingertips and your shoulder socket. Lengthen...

Dig your heels in

This exercise opens your hip joints and makes a strong connection between your heels and your pelvis.

From lying on your back, legs outstretched, feel your
heels as they rest against the surface of the floor.
Keeping your heels firmly on the floor, slide them
one at a time, toward your pelvis and away.
Concentrate on pressing into your heels as you
bend and straighten your knees, turning your legs
out and in, using wide legs, narrow legs.
Feel the awakening of your legs and hipjoints as you
dig your heels into the ground.

Dreamy head roll

This is an exercise about loosening the muscles of the neck and base of the skull.

Begin lying on your back with your eyes closed.
Feel the whole round volume of your head and its
contact with the floor.

Now, infinitesimally slowly, let your head begin to roll
to one side ... stopping several times along the way to
let the weight of your head sink into the floor.
Make it a very long journey ...
Keep going until your ear is facing the floor.
When you arrive there, breathe a deep sigh and let
all your tension spill out through your ear.
Then return to your starting position, taking time and
stops along the way as you did on the initial journey.

Before repeating the exercise to the other side
take time to feel the weight of your head resting
once again in the central position.

Tortoise stretch

To lengthen the back of the neck and release the shoulder muscles.

Begin in the folded position — sitting back on your heels — forehead and
forearms resting on the floor.

Breathe gently then
Slowly lift your head and like a
TORTOISE coming out of its shell
Lift your head out and up —
Keeping your neck long —
Arch away from the ground
Then
Exhale ... and sink
Floorwards into your shell again.

The snaking spine

On all fours the muscles of the spine can relax completely. The body weight is totally supported on the hands and knees.

Use the all fours position to loosen up your spine.

> Begin on your hands and knees.
> Let your belly relax completely, like a cat.
> Close your eyes and feel the whole spine from head to tail.
> Visualize the spine beginning to move like a snake in space.
> Imagine the small spinal joints deep inside you each moving separately within the snaking movement... move
> Slowly snaking up and down, side to side and all around.

> Rest by sitting back on your heels and resting your forehead on the floor. Breathe deeply. Then return to all fours and repeat the snaking movement.

Walking on air

> From lying down on your back
> 'WALK' your feet into the space around you
> Leave invisible footprints above, below and behind you.
> Use your heels, the balls of your feet, and toes

To reach as far as you can
Feel what is happening in the rest of
Your body
Roll, twist and stretch as you give your feet
More scope for
Air walking.

Waterfall hang

For lengthening the spine and releasing upper body tension.

Stand with the feet parallel and hips width apart, knees bent slightly

Let your head drop slowly forwards
Feel its weight
Pull you downwards...
Your head, shoulders, arms until
Your upper body hangs
Down towards the ground.

Exhale deeply
Imagine a waterfall
        running
           down
                your
                    back
Feel your spine lengthen
And your head loosen.

Then slowly from the base of your spine
Unfold upwards
Through the water —
Head up last — to stand
In the down rush of the
Waterfall.

Recognition of self

Through focusing on the body and movement, we may find a pathway toward making deeper contact with the Self. In all of us there is this unique essence that constitutes our individual personality or Self. We experience this essence in the body and through the body, but it is somehow deeper, greater than our physical selves.

Hopefully you will consciously experience all the exercises in the book through your own unique personal awareness . . . "this is me moving . . . what I feel is being experienced and expressed through my own individual Self".

 Movement, after all, is not separate from the rest of life. Through movement you can find ways to use your energy, your strength, your sensitivity to function and to express all aspects of yourself. To give out and to take in. By allowing your feelings, your sensations, your tendencies, you accept yourself. In moving, you define yourself.

It is through this experience of the individuality of Self that we may be more likely to recognize our unity with all living things.

SUMMARY — LENGTHENING AND LOOSENING

In this section we have worked with the material of the body, enjoying

- deep body stretches
- reaching out into the space
- lengthening, twisting, curling
- opening the body

We have followed a flow of awareness through the body . . . beginning to gain a deeper sense of ourselves through movement.

"Dancing is motion, the conversion of inner, invisible animation into bodily movement."

Mary Wigman
The Mary Wigman Book

5

MOVEABLE PARTS

In this section the exercises focus in deeply on specific parts or areas of the body. You will get a feeling for the way the different joints of the skeleton work, the way parts function in relation to each other, and the way movement follows through from one part of the body to another.

Explore these exercises with a sense of fun and curiosity to feel all the various moveable parts, and how they work both separately and together.

You may find it useful to refer back to the section on 'Self massage' (pages 19–21). Self massage is a useful way of warming and sensitizing parts of the body before using them in movement.

Upper body — lower body

Explore the contrasting movement qualities of the upper and lower body, with an awareness of their connection through the waist.

> Standing, anchored by feet and legs
> Explore the movement of your
> Upper body
> Use twisting, stretching, opening
> And closing. Move out and away
> With large, space eating gestures.
> Discover the expressive power
> Of your arms, hands, head and torso.
>
> Then use only your pelvis, legs and feet,
> Twisting, thrusting downwards,
> Stamping and gesturing,
> Enliven your lower body.
>
> Imagine your upper body as airborne
> And your lower as earth grounded
> And find a flow of movement

> Spiralling, dynamically
> From one to the other.

It is interesting to explore upper and lower body movement from lying down too. Released from the necessity of keeping you balanced upright, the lower body can move more freely.

Lower back roll

> Lie on your back
> Knees folded up to your chest
> Arms flopped out
> You can stay like this forever.
>
> Now let your knees gently
> Sink to the floor on one side
> Leaving your shoulders
> Where they are.
> Breathe into this twist in your spine.
>
> Then slowly roll back across your pelvis
> Knees floating back to centre
> Settle there...
> Then repeat the movement to the
> Other side.
>
> Then with your knees together
> Take them round in a gentle circle
> One way then the other.

Use this exercise to give your lower back a massage.

Seven regions

From lying comfortably, with knees bent or legs outstretched, use your hands to locate each region and then focus your attention by breathing into it and letting the place feel itself... not only on the surface but deep inside.

Stay with each position as long as you like. Feel free to explore working with them in a different order.

1. **PELVIS** — Place the heels of both hands on your hipbones. Let your fingers rest on the lower belly. Breathe into your pelvis.

2. **WAIST** — Rest your hands on your waist. Be aware of the soft space between ribs and pelvis.
3. **SOLAR PLEXUS** — Rest your hands on your solar plexus, the soft triangle at the bottom of your ribcage.
4. **HEART** — Open your fingers wide and rest them on your upper chest. Let your breath radiate out from your heart in all directions.
5. **THROAT** — Circle your neck lightly with your fingers. Breathe into the column of your throat.
6. **JAW** — Cup your jaw with your hands, fingers fanning lightly across your cheeks. Let your jaw relax down into your hands as you exhale.
7. **SKULL** — Rest relaxed hands on your skull. Send your breath all the way to the top.

Bubbling up the spine

This exercise focuses on every part of your spine especially the tailbone. Touch it before you begin to help your awareness.

> From lying, begin a small circling movement
> With the very end of your tailbone.
> Once in the groove of this tiny movement,
> Almost more a thought than a movement,
> Allow this circling to move along your spine
> Like bubbles rising through the vertebrae,
> All the way to the top of your head and
> Beyond it into circling energy.

A figure eighting spine

From standing, draw a figure eight with your tailbone. Let this movement grow in your body and in the space until your arms and spine and head and even your legs are involved in the free flow swoops and curves of the movement.

Spine information

Our health and well being are directly related to the state of our spines. The spine is the central part of our bony framework and is the corridor through which our central nervous system links all parts of our body. In movement it

is versatile, but prone to stress and disturbance, being both affected by and
influencing all the rest of the body. Our breathing is directly connected to the
movement of our spines. Our spines literally move as we breathe. Through
movement and visualization, we can help our spines to stay ... balanced
                                                              lengthened
                                                              flexible and
                                                              expressive.

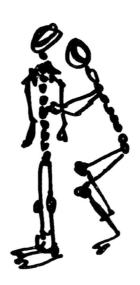

Orchestrating the trunk

The spine is the central support for the trunk, for the volumes of the
pelvis ... the ribcage ... and the head. In this exercise move these three parts
independently and then altogether.

    Begin standing, eyes closed.
    Sense where each of the three volumes joins the spine.
    Begin to explore movement with the pelvis,
    Then the ribcage, and then the head
    Using movements of forward and back, sideways, around.
    Experience moving each part in isolation.

    Then, like an orchestra tuning up, let these
    sections move freely as they wish.
    Keep an overview of the whole,

The three parts moving in relation to each other.
Feel your spine at the core of the movement,
Harmoniously holding it all together.

Head to floor massage

On hands and knees with elbows bent
Rest the very top of your head on the floor
Relax your neck. Feel the weight of your head.
Then slowly roll your head backwards and forwards
Side to side — roll all over the
Surface of your skull. Feel the bones.
Allow the floor to massage you.

Then sit back
Hold your head between the palms of your hands
Feel the warmth and shape of your head.
Press or circle into the scalp a little
And then lightly brush the hands
Over the head, down the back of the neck
And off the shoulders to finish.

Where the skull meets the spine

Get in touch with the place where your skull meets your spine. This is often
a key place of tension and compression.

Trace and encase

Starting just behind your ears,
Trace round the base of your skull with your thumbs.

Then place both hands over your skull
Encasing it snugly.
Rest here a moment.
Visualize your skull.

The small yes–no

Locate the hollow at the base of your skull and
Using your index finger, initiate a tiny nodding movement,
A small 'yes' and then a small 'no'.
Feel how only your head moves,
Independently of your spine.
Create more space in the joint.
Picture your head floating light and free.

Freely arcing head

Gently encase your head with your hands.
Begin to guide yourself in a head-led journey.
Allow yourself to follow wherever your head leads you.
Pass your head from one hand to the other.
Take it forward and backward
Arcing and dipping and rotating
Extending into space.

Try these exercises with a partner. It's nice having someone else give you the cues.

Oiling the hip joint

Lubricate the hip joint with warmth through movement

Lie on your back and
Fold in one knee
Mobilize the hip joint gently
By moving the knee in circles
With your hand.

Focus on how the hip socket feels
Circle into any stiff parts
Change the direction of the movement.

To finish, give your leg a long stretch out
And slide it down softly to the floor
Again.

Try this exercise without supporting your knee with your hands and thereby increasing its range of movement. Perhaps add stretching the leg in different directions as a further development.

Improvisation arising from an exercise

When working from any specific sequence of movement, you may wish to develop from there into simple improvisation; or, if the exercise already incorporates an improvisatory element, you can enlarge upon that. If you are genuinely deeply focussed on a particular movement sequence, you will begin to sense other possibilities arising from it. Follow the feeling in your body. The movement may involve more parts of your body, or another movement might be added to the exercise. In this way you could choose to add to and play with the original idea.

Barefoot thoughts

Our feet connect us to the earth. Through our feet we feel the ground beneath us. But encased in shoes we cut off a vital part of our body's sensitivity. Barefoot we can feel connected to stone, grass, carpet, water, sand.

Walking on different surfaces teaches us about our feet, as they respond to changes of temperature and texture. If you vitalize your feet, you enliven yourself. There is a distinct link between how your feet feel and how you feel. Find again the sensations of barefoot childhood.

Four foot exercises

Splay

Stand, splay your toes wide
Then grip them inwards, like grabbing a footful of sand.
Splay and grip — splay and grip
Splay and
Walk
Feeling the backs of your toes on the ground.

Swivel

> Try foot swivels.
> Lift the heel of one foot
> and swivel the ball about.
> From feet flat, swivel your heels.
> Then rest on your heels and
> Scissor your feet.

Tiptoe

> Stand on tip toes
> Walk on the balls of your feet
> Then walk on the heels.
> Walk on the outsides of your feet,
> Then on the insides.

Steps

> Find your stepping power...
> Hops, jumps, skips, kicks
> Gallop steps and leaps
> Mix them and mould them
> Into bursts of high energy
> Or light foot tapping phrases.
> Listen to the rhythm of your feet.

Foot massage

Get to know your feet more deeply, all the joints, bones, tendons and textures.

> Hold your foot with warm hands
> Just hold it and give it some comfort
> Between the palms of your hands.
>
> Then gently explore with your fingers and palms
> The contours, the soft and hard parts
> Press and stroke and knead your foot,
> Using circling movements with your thumb,
> Search for sore places.
>
> Encourage the foot to widen.
> Spread the bones of the foot outward.
> Massage each toe separately,
> So that each one has a life of its own.
> Squeeze the heel.
> Pinch along the achilles tendon.
> Feel your whole foot begin to soften and breathe.

Before repeating on the other side, observe the difference in feeling between your two feet. Be kind to your feet. You won't be going anywhere without them.

Moon walks

> Carefully place your feet in
> Slow motion walks
> Sense your weight
> Rising and sinking
> Settling and turning
> Follow your articulate feet.
>
> Be aware of each slow transfer of
> Weight from foot to foot . . .
> Through the heel into the ball and toes
> The weight rolling onto the
> Front foot as it peels off
> The back foot.
>
> Feel the changing design
> Of your whole body as you

Explore the subtleties of
Slow moon walking.

Seaweed arms

From lying on your back
Lift your arms above you
Twist and turn and float
Them through the space
Move from the shoulders
The elbows wrists and fingers
A-r-t-i-c-u-l-a-t-e
Imagine your joints
Floating in the water
Imagine the spaces
Between your bones.

Then play with the same idea but now from standing.

Angels in the snow

Lie down on your back and as you extend into this full arm movement feel the connection between your shoulder blades and your arms.

Like children making angels in the snow,
Slide your arms out and upwards along the ground,
with your thumbs leading the way,
till they meet above your head.

Then, slowly return along the same path,
carving a groove through the snow.
Extend into this movement again and again.

Homage to the hands

Hands are wonderfully complex. We use them for giving, grasping, grappling, comforting, caressing, pushing, poking ... expressing nuances of meaning and manipulating the environment to carry out wishes and work. Hands are superbly functional and creative mechanisms.

Three hand exercises

Rippling

> Begin with strong outstretched hands and fingers.
> Then press forward slowly like cat paws kneading
> and ripple through wrists, palms and fingers,
> Curving them around into soft fists
> and outstretching again.
> Repeat the movement many times
> to strengthen and articulate the hands.

Finger fan

> From fisted fingers
> Both hands at once, open and stretch
> Thumb, index, middle, ring, pinky
> Fingers stretching wide as you can.
> Then reversing, close them
> Pinky, ring, middle, index, thumb
> Repeat many times
> To stretch and enliven your hands.

Hand designs

> Find hand designs through contact of
> Fingers, wrists, backs of the hands, palms —
> Play with hand gestures —
> Rotating the wrists, stretching the fingers
> Play with two hands touching
> Through many permutations in
> Slow changes of shape and feeling.

> Sometimes move only the hands
> Sometimes allow the body to follow
> Becoming part of the design
> Hands can move away from the body and back
> Like birds moving and settling.

Where to begin

Our movement is clearer if we know where in the body the movement begins.

> Lead your movement with one body part at a time.
> Try letting your hand begin to carve through space
> And the rest of your body follows.
> Or try starting with the top of your head.
> See where this parts leads you and
> Let the rest of your body follow
> In a free flowing dance.
> Transitioning from one part leading to another
> May be an especially significant moment.
> Feel your many-faceted body.
> As you move through space.

This could be the beginning of a dance; or share it with a partner in a gamelike way, calling out the leading body parts to each other.

Wall moves

> Stand with your back against a wall
> Then without losing contact
> Slowly change your body position
> Move into different two dimensional
> Body shapes.
>
> Lean into the wall and feel
> How it supports you
> So you can play with
> Instigating movement
> From different body parts
> Be adventurous
> Go to the limits of your flexibility.
>
> While staying in contact
> With the wall
> Visualize the designs
> That you make as you move against it.

Release into movement

> Stand in complete stillness and from there
> Recognize any tight and holding places in your body
> Then release these into movement — let them
> Fall, loosen, shake or swing, then
> Pause when you like in any position
> Make each stillness a recognition point
> For where you are holding onto yourself
> Before moving again.
>
> Discover how you want to move
> Through listening to your body
> Free yourself into movement.

Connect up

> Choose two parts of your body
> and play with connecting them in movement
> Perhaps two parts which feel less aware and alive
> like the back of your head and your heel
> or your shoulder blade and your hip joint.

Be aware of the changing shapes and moods of your body as you explore
these connections.

SUMMARY — MOVEABLE PARTS

In this section, as you focus in deeply into a specific body part, you may find that your awareness of the whole body increases.

Exploring   – joints
                             – parts, and
                             – connections

within your three-dimensional self.

After becoming familiar with the exercises, you may intuitively combine them, finding a dancing pathway from one to another to another.

*"And as a single leaf turns not yellow
but with the silent knowledge of the whole tree."*

Kahlil Gibran
The Prophet

6

FINDING BODY RHYTHMS

There are innumerable natural rhythms happening in the body: pulse, breath, digestive impulse, heartbeat, most of which we are not tuned into most of the time. Likewise, the impulse to move creates body rhythms, rhythmic patterns which combine a subtle blend of long and short phrases, accents, changes of pace, pauses and stillness. Try developing an awareness of your personal rhythmic patterns and the way you pace yourself in movement. You may discover something about how you experience time in your life.

"I'm a staccato sort of person. I'm always starting and stopping."
"I'm like a snail sometimes. It's hard to get going at all."
"There's an underlying feeling of always hurrying to get things done."

The breath and the heartbeat

There are rhythmic patterns within you even when you are completely still. The most obvious ones are the breathing and the heartbeat which exist as two separate but simultaneous rhythms within you. When you are still you can become aware of the involuntary movements within the body.

> Close your eyes for a few moments
> Simply listen to and feel these two rhythms
> First the breath . . . the pattern of inhale and exhale
> Then the heartbeat . . . the tempo of its pulse . . . the
> feel of it in other parts of your body.
> Concentrate on both the breath and the heartbeat
> at the same time.
> Feel the different rhythmic quality of each.
>
> Then gradually take the rhythm into movement.
> Concentrate on doing two things at once.
> Moving to the heartbeat and to the breath.

> Using different parts of your body at the same time,
> Perhaps feet pulsing ... arms breathing.

Try to shut out all other noise, both outside and inside your head. Be totally involved with the inaudible music of your own internal rhythms.

Phrasing through breath

Movement like music occurs in phrases. A phrase is a pathway from one point of stillness to another. The following exercise explores phrasing and its natural relationship to breathing. You can use your breath to support your phrasing and to help punctuate your movement.

> Move freely, spontaneously
> Making phrases of movement
> Long ones, short ones ...
> Consider accents,
> Gathering or losing energy,
> Exploding, lilting, falling ...
>
> Then let your breathing support or create
> the rhythmic patterns of your movement.
> Move along a long drawn out breath,
> The sound of a sharp intake,
> or a measured inhale and exhale.
> Movement and breath
> A reciprocal relationship.

Notice how the breath is the tell-tale feature which lets you know how fully you allow yourself to be involved.

> *Keeping time*
> *Keeping the rhythm in their dancing*
> *As in their living in the living seasons*

T. S. Eliot
The Four Quartets

Playing with repetition

> Through easy, unforced repetition of a movement phrase
> Its rhythmic quality grows and develops

It takes on a life of its own,
The rhythm infusing and enlivening the movement.
The energy may change like shades of colour
The movement may become delicate or very strong
It may speed up urgently or gently slow down
The movement may grow in size or shrink
or may fly, fling away, for a moment out of control
And then be gathered in, carefully shaped and defined once more.

Discover how a repeated phrase changes and develops quite unconsciously without deliberately deciding how it will do so. Just go with the ever changing flow.

Of course there is a place for exact repetition of the rhythm and movement of a particular phrase. Through exact repetition you can become aware of every nuance.

See 'Inner intention' (page 37)

Spontaneous response to music

Instead of taking the impulse to move from inside yourself, use music as a catalyst to draw you into movement, to awaken your own rhythmic sense.

Respond freely to the rhythm
of the music
in your movement.
Follow the pattern of the music
or weave your own pattern . . .
quickening, slowing, pausing,
Moving in and out of the music.
A dynamic co-existence
of music and movement.

Use different kinds of music to externalize different moods, to spark your imagination or touch your emotions.

Spontaneous response to a partner

Try taking on the rhythms of another person, either as you both respond to music or as you move in silence following your rhythmic impulses. This gives you the chance to experience rhythms which are not your natural choice. Extend yourself beyond your habitual rhythmic patterns.

"Your rhythms enlivened me. It was enormously regenerating".
"It was a relief not to have to be responsible for being creative every moment.
I'd just look at your movement and immediately pick up something to get me in-
volved again".

Rhythms of relating

Extend your ways of dancing with a partner. One person begins moving
freely. The other observes for a time then joins in one of the following ways:

Unison or mirror
An exact replica of your partner

Agreement
Share the same style, the same energy or rhythmic pattern, but not necessarily the same movement

Opposition
A sharp contrast with your partner's movement

Conversation
Respond to each other in movement as you would in a spoken dialogue

Exaggeration
Enlarge on some aspect of your partner's movement

Contact
Move in physical contact with your partner. See 'Making contact' (page 81)

Pause your dance after a time to share and discuss the feelings, images and
fantasies that may arise, and perhaps incorporate these into your dance.

Stillness or movement

Stillness and movement are like the opposite sides of a coin. Stillness is just
as much a part of rhythm as movement. The experience of one will heighten
the experience of the other. Movement without moments of stillness can become a sort of 'body chatter'.

Use stillness to listen to and respond to your body, to reflect on your movement and to give breathing spaces.

Two opposite exercises

1. Move continuously, fast or slow
   Creating your own rhythmic phrases
   Then introduce long pauses into the
   flow of movement
   Patches where you are motionless
   Suspended in time.

2. Choose a kneeling, sitting or standing
   starting position.
   Stay quite still until you have a
   Strong impulse to move
   any way you choose
   To arrive again into another sculpted stillness.

The first exercise is punctuated by stillness, the second by movement. Compare how they feel to you.

The present moment

> *What is my present moment*
> *It is the sounds that I hear*
> *Now in this instant, the*
> *Temperature of the air*
> *Around me, the position I am*
> *In and the feeling in my*
> *Body.*
> *The present moment is always*
> *Moving into the past but if I do not*
> *Experience it I am like a*
> *Paper person blowing in the*
> *Wind.*

R. S.

By deepening our experience of each moment we strengthen ourselves for the time to follow. By enriching our sense of the present, we do not have to be so anxious or controlling of what happens next and so leave ourselves open to unexpectedness, surprise and pleasure. When you are dancing alone or with a partner, allow yourself to savour the moments of balance and resting as well as the pattern of movement. Often you do not know what is to happen next, so allow yourself to wait. Wait and it will happen through you.

SUMMARY — FINDING BODY RHYTHMS

Rhythm is fundamental to movement. It is of the essence of our being. Through our body rhythms, we express our internal world and respond to the outer world. Through our moment to moment experience of time, we form our intuitive rhythmic expression, which can be compared to a non-verbal language. We elucidate this through focussing on

– breath and heartbeat
– phrasing and repetition
– stillness and movement

to re-awaken ourselves to the joy and meaning of rhythm.

"Unquestionably the conception of time as a fixed present and as pure actuality is more ancient than that of chronometric time, which is not an immediate apprehension of the flow of reality but is instead a rationalization of its passing."

Octavio Paz
The Labyrinth of Solitude

7

SENSING AND SEEING

Sensing and seeing involves receiving information on a non-verbal level. We focus on the tactile and the visual, with inner seeing being equally as powerful as literal seeing; in one way using the eyes to look outwards at our surroundings, and in another way seeing with the inner eye through the use of visualization. And similarly, the idea of "sensing" is related both to our body awareness and to the opening of all the senses to receive impressions.

We encourage you to respond to what is already there in your body and your mind. Even the most subtle awareness can be a point of departure for further exploration.

The outer layer

Who am I in this
World behind my skin
Into my bones into the
Very depth of me.

Skin

You are enclosed by it
It is your first contact
With the world around you
It wraps around every part of you
Inside and out
To protect you and inform you
About the external environment
It forms a tactile boundary
Between you and the world
Dwell on the image of yourself
Inside your skin.

Sensing through touch

Sensing through touch is like "seeing" and "listening" through the skin. With practice you can become more aware of your sense of touch.

Try simply placing your hands on your own body and notice its warmth, skin texture and the underlying muscle and bone. Be aware of the experience of both touching and being touched.

In a similar way you can experience another person, receiving "messages" about who they are and how they feel both emotionally and physically, being aware simultaneously of the other person and yourself.

Back sensing with a partner

In this exercise one person receives the touch of another. To prepare yourself before sensing your partner, rub your hands together and place them on your stomach just below your navel and breathe into them there to focus your energy.

> Partner A lie comfortably on your front
> Breathe gently. Relax.
>
> Partner B gently place your hands
> Across your partner's shoulders
> And slowly move your hands
> Down and over your partner's back.
>
> Discover part by part —
> Shoulder blades — upper back — ribs —
> Waist and back of the pelvis.
>
> Touch gently and pause
> Wait in reflective stillness and
> Listen through the
> Palms of your hands.
>
> Allow your hands to guide you
> To soft or hard places
> To feel the body shape, to be
> Aware of breath.

Share with each other your feelings and thoughts about this experience, how it feels to touch and to be touched. Then repeat this exercise, switching roles.

Tracing

> Define the shape of your face
> By tracing feather light with finger tips
> Over all its surface, aware of
> Skin sensation.
>
> Then trace along the outer shape
> Of your whole body
> Visualize your shape as you "draw" around
> The outline of yourself —
> Skull shape, shoulders, around each
> Finger, and on the way
> Feel curves and contours, indentations
> And textures
> Imagine the secret life of your body
> Hidden beneath the skin.
>
> Try tracing with a partner,
> Outlining your partner by the light touch of
> Gentle tracing, with the finger tips
> Or feet or any body part,
> Reciprocal tracing, defining
> Each others shape
> Instigating movement or outlining the
> Stillness.

Breathing pathways

From lying, sitting or standing use your "inner eye" to visualize these breathing pathways. Seeing inward, focus your breathing to fill out your sense of three-dimensional body space. Repeat each cycle several times.

> First breathe into *length,*
> Growing along the spine
> Both upward and downward as you inhale
> On the exhale release back slightly
> Toward centre.
>
> Breathe into *width* by widening on the inhale
> Breathing into both sides of your body.
> On the exhale narrow back toward centre.

Breathe into *depth*
Filling the space
Between front and back.
On the exhale hollow in
Toward the spine.

Extend this exercise by varying the directions as you like. Notice which feel most accessible, which are least familiar.

Getting a feel for space

Space is the medium we move in. Movement makes the space come alive. Think of space not as a blank, invisible void, but as a substance. Feel it. Feel your movement cut through space and define it.

Begin with one hand only
Watch your hand as you gather space toward your body
And then open the fingers to push space away.
Let your other hand join in this carving action.
Imagine your movements leaving trace patterns in the space.
Feel and see simultaneously.

As your hands become sensitive to the feel of space, let the movement grow, working through to the elbow, then the whole arm. Try the same idea starting with other body parts. Begin with a foot, then feel the whole leg carve through space.

Or try it with the top of your head. Each time develop the movement right into your whole body.

Taking shape

These exercises are about creating body shapes. The first is inner-focussed and the second is focussed out. Compare the difference in feeling you have in these two ways of working.

Inner shaping

Beginning in any position
With eyes closed, but inner eyes open

Feel the inside mass and space of your body
Imagine it boneless, formless, amoeba-like
With the impulse coming from a desire to mould this shape,
Begin to let yourself ooze around
Down, up, lengthen, condense, grow, shrink, hollow, bulge
An organic flow of moving breathing shapes.

Outer shaping

This time your focus is on the outer space
So keep your eyes wide open. *See* the space,
Mould it with your hands, arms, torso, legs, head.
As you carve and shape space in this way
You change and mould your body shape.
Move through the room shaping your way.

In both ways of working you may wish to pause in stillness from time to time
to experience your shape from the inside or out. Try changing your focus
mid-stream, from inner shaping to outer shaping. Can your focus flow freely
from one to the other?

Fresh eyes

A baby moves in response to what she perceives around her — shapes,
colours, familiar faces. Her eyes lead her into reaching out, pushing up, rolling over to explore the world.

She has no name for anything as yet, so her visual response is very pure. The
following exercise is designed to rediscover this innocent way of looking.

From foetal lying, close your eyes and
focus on relaxing the muscles behind and around your eyes.
Let your face muscles relax.
Then open your eyes, softly taking in your view.
Use your eyes to lead you
into slow head movement.
Curiosity to explore motivates the head
Turning and twisting in all directions.
Gradually let your whole body become involved
in following the gentle scanning of your eyes
Up, down, behind, around you.

Forest and the trees

Try this exercise to experience two different ways of focusing your eyes.

First focus on something near you.
Inspect it. See all the details.
Then look at something else.
Zero in, scrutinizing.
Do this many times.

Now try slightly defocusing your eyes.
Emphasize your peripheral vision.
Don't focus on any one thing.
Take in everything.

Then walk about using these modes of perception.
Zeroing in, seeing the details.
Then defocusing again, seeing the overview.
Go back and forth.
Notice the difference in feeling in both your body
and your mind in these two modes of seeing.

Sound space

Begin in stillness
Focus on the sounds you hear
all around you
Sense the direction and distance of sounds
from where you are

Sense the whole sphere of surrounding space
coloured by sounds
Try absorbing the sounds
into your body ...

And then
Begin to move in this sound space
Let the sound touch you
inspire you
quiet your thoughts
and connect you to a larger world

Try this exercise both indoors and out. Also, explore working with eyes
closed or open. Perhaps you will wish to add some sounds of your own.

Using imagery

Visual images can heighten body awareness and evoke spontaneous movement. A particular image may be chosen as a starting point for movement or
imagery may arise from movement itself. So we can think of imagery as being
guided (suggested) or arising unexpectedly from the unconscious. Both ana-
tomical and fantasy images have the power to produce subtle physical and
emotional changes in our bodies, e.g. an image may help us to lengthen, release tight parts, to soften or expand.

> Images are like internal photographs
> Dreamlike they float into our minds . . .
> Objects, colours, shapes, real or
> Imagined landscapes, symbolic of our
> Thoughts and feelings.

Sometimes one, sometimes a series of these dreamlike photographs will become part of a movement experience. Each person's experience of an image
will be unique and each person's response will be different.

From image to movement

Choose an image, one from the examples in this section or make up one of
your own. Lie, sit or stand in a comfortable position and close your eyes.

> Hold the image in your mind.
> See it, feel it, breathe it into you.
> First be in a state of not knowing
> what is going to happen.
> Step right into the image and
> Let it take you into movement.
> A spontaneous, intuitive response to the image.
> Don't stop to analyze or edit.
> You may "become" your image or
> move in relationship to it.
> Ride the image for as long as it moves you.
> It may come, go, change, develop
> as you work with it and it works with you.

Through movement you have a tangible expression of your image and feeling. The interplay between image to movement to image is constantly fluid.

Examples of images for movement

Try responding spontaneously to any of these images, or try creating your
own list of images through free association, on your own or with a partner.

> Shoulder blades softening and hanging —
> The head is a helium balloon —
> Feet like pancakes or feet like talons —
> Arms like seaweed or arms like swords —
> Spine like a snake
>
> Waterfall
> thick mud
> honey
> hot coals
> tree tops
> feathers
> thunder

spray on the waves
a pig shaped cloud
a black vortex
shining ice
a broken umbrella
sidewalks at midnight
footsteps in the sand

These images may relate to body parts or body shape, to movement qualities, to rhythm or mood, to any aspect of movement that you choose.

Energy current

Imagine an
Electric current moves
Within you
Transmitting movement connections
Sparking the
Energy from one body part
To another to
Create a moving ENERGY FIELD.

Kite

Flying, dipping, tugging, falling
Aspiring upwards
Changeable in mood
Airborne with the wind while
Tethered to the earth.

From movement to image

In this exercise you start with movement itself with the intention of finding out what associated images will arise.

The only way to begin is to begin
Whatever you feel like doing —
Rocking, twisting, walking
Or touching the surrounding space...
Choose some movements

Allow them to be a key
To your unconscious
Let an image
Enter.
Choose an image for the
Space or
A part of your body or
An emotion you are feeling
Allow a tide of image and movement
To flood through you.

Some of your most significant images may occur in this spontaneous and unexpected way. They can be used there and then as part of the movement experience and also noted and stored for future use.

Responses — images arising from movement

The following responses arose from people working with this process of movement → image → movement:

"My spine is moving fluidly. The sea has entered my bones".

"My spine is glowing, extending the limits of my body".

"The whole world is orange. There is no boundary between my skin and the orange world".

"My shoulder blades feel like wings".

"The sun is inside me radiating down my arms and legs".

"I have an image of spaghetti. It really softens my bones and muscles".

"I have bright yellow in my feet. I stamp and bounce — bright yellow floods my head and makes me laugh".

"I have an image of a snake coiling inside me. It feels really painful".

"I am moving through a fragile web".

These may equally well be used as starting points for movement for oneself or to stimulate others, e.g., imagine your body as spaghetti.

Being moved by images

As we allow ourselves to move freely with the imagery, not trying to exert control on everything that happens and accepting the unexpected, we may experience the freeing sensation of "being moved", where we have given up our conscious volition and decision making in movement and opened ourselves to whatever may happen. Not "out of control" but not "controlling" the movement.

Through movement we accept and form the reality of the unconscious, allowing images to have a power and value of their own, not following a rational logic.

Imagery is used in different contexts throughout the book, but the following group of exercises focus specifically on the use of imagery as a starting point, either to create subtle sensations of response in your body or to lead you directly into movement.

Unzipping yourself

An image for centering yourself and for developing an awareness of the right and left halves of your body.

> Lie on your back and close your eyes.
> Focus your attention on your spine,
> A string of moveable bones
> Dividing your left side from your right.
>
> Observe any difference between the two sides.
> Does one leg feel longer? Is one shoulder higher?
> One hip higher? One eye more contracted?
> These differences may feel very large,
> Like looking at something through a magnifying glass.
>
> Now try slowly U-N-Z-I-P-P-I-N-G your spine
> Right from the top to the bottom.
> Feel yourself lengthening and widening
> As your spine responds to the image.

Spine moves

> Do you know what your
> Spine looks like?
> Imagine the length of it
> From the base
> Right up to
> Behind your eyes, twenty six

Vertebrae — imagine air around
Each one.

Sense the back of your spine
And the front
Sense the thickness of it.

Now take the image into movement
Through walking, hanging down, kneeling
Or rolling
"Watch" the movement of
Your spine.

Let it be tranquil, playful or
Violent, feel its power
Then rest it like a
Languid snake upon the ground.

Body curves

Consider all the curves in the body
Find connections between the heel,
The arch of the foot and the curve of the skull,
The rim of the pelvis
The round cage of the ribs
And the curves of the hip joint.

In your mind identify these places
Feel them with your hands
Imagine what they look like
Then, take your time and
Begin to move.
Let your thoughts curve into your body
Let your body curve into your thoughts.

Then focussing into the space around you, move into

A curving dance

Explore body curving movements
Draw curving lines around you
Use the inside of your arm

Your elbow and the
Palms of your hands ...
Arch your spine
Curl over into a foetal curve
Trace crescent moons with the top of
Your head, circle your sacrum
Enjoy, repeat, define these movements
Into a curving dance.

Power points

Visualize these points and focus your attention first on your lower body centre and then your upper body centre. These points "centre you" deeply
within yourself.

Lower centre point

To find the lower centre point
Visualize it in the middle of your pelvis
in front of your spine and
just below your navel.
This is also the centre of gravity of your body.

Place your hands over the centre point
Imagine it as a tiny coloured light
deep inside you.
Breathe into it.
See and feel this centre point.

Upper centre point

To find the upper centre point,
Visualize it deep inside your chest
Underneath the sternum bone.
You would point here when you point to yourself.
Place your hands there
See this point as a coloured light
Glowing inside you.

On another level these two centres relate to emotional feelings, to gut level reactions and heartfelt expression. After locating these places, try moving from the centre points and feeling the different qualities of the two, and the different moods and actions they lead you into.

Images for grounding through the feet

> Imagine the nerve endings in your feet
> Waking up, lighting up
> Opening channels of communication
> Between your feet and the Earth.
>
> Imagine your feet like a three-pronged plug.
> Plug yourself into the Earth.
> One prong at the big toe, one at the little toe
> and a third in the heel.
> A strong connection.
>
> Imagine diagonal energy lines across the soles of your feet.
> A line from big toe to outside of heel and
> one from little toe to inside of heel.
> Lengthen and stabilize along these lines
> Visualize the X where the two lines intersect.
> Use this as a centring point for aligning your whole body.

Head thoughts

> From sitting or standing
> Imagine your head is floating
> Just attached by a fine thread
> To your body
> Fill your head with a light, floating colour.
>
> Then visualize your head moving gently
> Into the space around you
> Trailing your spine
> Like a ribbon.
>
> Gradually begin to move
> Hum a twining melody to
> Accompany your head led dance.

Eyes closed — eyes open

In some exercises in the book you are directed to work either with eyes open
or closed. In others the choice is yours. Try experimenting with combining
the two, eyes open for a while, then closed. Try working with eyes fraction-
ally open, as if you are seeing through a haze of eyelashes. Experience the
differences. Which feels better to you?

> With eyes closed
> As if you are blind
> Or moving in complete darkness
> Allow your limbs to become like
> Super sensitive antennae.
> Feel the space around
> As tangible, amorphous
> Like a dark sea.
>
> Be aware of your body, its shape,
> Slow pace and quickening,
> Be bold. Step into the unknown.
>
> Then with eyes open,
> Experience the light, look around
> Let your body follow the movement
> Of your eyes
> As you scan your surroundings.
>
> As you move in response to
> The visible outer world
> Feel yourself drawn into space
> Reaching to new directions
> Keep a connection between
> Seeing, breathing, and inner sensation.
>
> Eyes closed, eyes open
> Two different perceptions of
> Yourself.

The experience of moving with your eyes closed allows you to focus attention on the subtle inner sensations of the body, and the related emotional
associations, memories or images which may spontaneously arise.

With eyes open, the surroundings may take precedence. Using
the eyes induces a more alert state of mind. The focus is outward taking

in the space around you. There may tend to be greater attention to the form of your movement and a stronger intention to communicate to others.

Try keeping a flow of awareness between outer and inner seeing.

SUMMARY — SENSING AND SEEING

In this section, we make use of the imagination as well as the senses, the physical sources of perception, as catalysts for movement. We have looked at the transformative power of the image and the way that movement is related simultaneously to our experience of the outside world as well as to our physical sensation.

By responding to
               – space
               – image
               – seeing
               – hearing
               – touching

"With eyes open to three dimensions and bodies caught in time, the fourth, most of us are asleep to imagination, the fifth, and its workings show themselves only dimly in our dreams."

Stephen Larsen
Shaman's Doorway

8

MAKING CONTACT

Moving in contact with a partner can bring us more in contact with our-selves. With a partner you are freed of the need to always initiate movement by yourself. You can share the responsibility. In moving together you begin to communicate with each other, and in so doing you may find that you extend yourself beyond your individual range of movement. Together you can take risks and investigate unknown territory.

Many exercises in the book may be developed into partner work, some of which have been directly indicated. 'Rhythms of relating' (page 60) gives you many suggestions for ways to proceed.

We focus now on exercises which are specifically using physical con-tact with a partner.

Guidelines for partner work

To help you feel more relaxed and confident in your interplay:

Take time to feel comfortable in your starting position.

Try to sense any undue effort coming from you or your partner. Do not work against tension.

Try to communicate non-verbally through sensing and "listening" rather than through words.

Note how you share the energy, give and take, merge and adapt.

Develop a feeling for how long you want to move. Continue for as long or as short a time as you wish.

Back to back

Sit back to back with a partner
Lean together with whole spines merging

With eyes closed sense the contact between you
Just breathe into this connection for awhile . . .
The weight and the warmth . . .
And feel a subtle flow of movement begin.
Supporting and leaning,
Feel the give and take of weight.
Let the contact grow and go where it will,
Pressing and shifting,
Communicate with your partner through
Flexible, sensitive spines.
Discover your partner's back through your own.

Counter balance

Begin facing your partner an arm's length apart, gently holding each other's
wrists with your arms relaxed, feet straight ahead and knees flexed.

Gradually straighten your arms and
Lean away from each other.
Hold each other's weight
through stretched but relaxed arms.
Without this support
you would
fall over
backwards.

Then sink toward a squatting position.
Feel the stretch in your spine.
Take it easy . . . do not strain.

Then on the way up try
turning your body, undulating through your spine,

shifting your feet or
holding with one hand only.
Keep leaning away.
Trust your partner
to support you.

After this specific exercise try improvising with the following one.

Stretching with a partner

Use your partner to help you stretch
Through finding ways to link and hook together
To support you in movements you could not do alone.
Try leaning into hanging away
Pulling and extending each other
Use the point of contact between you as a focus
To stretch away from and press into to find
A variety of supported and extended body shapes.
Feel the movement radiating from your contact.
Leave each other and return at will.

My weight, your weight

We often lose touch with the sensation of our own weight. As we experience
"letting go", we may realize how much we were holding onto ourselves.
Working with a partner, giving or taking weight we can experience many
subtle gradations of physical sensation.

Stand a little apart, back to back
Gently lean into each other to
Establish two spines joined in total contact.
Feel the strength in your legs
The mutual support
Feel your partner's breathing.
Stay still until the moment
For moving arrives.
Then keeping contact and
Slowly rolling your weight across each other
Move till you contact in a new position
Head to shoulder perhaps...

Sliding downwards, head to knee...
Find your own pace and rhythm
Discover resting places
Experience mutual support.

"I felt very strong. My spine felt like your spine. My arms felt light. We were like a sea creature with tentacles. I recognized which parts of me were passive and hanging, and which were actively supporting me".

Felt messages

Massaging a partner can lead quite easily into a form of contact dance. Touch and pressure can be like signals for movement. We can interchange giving or receiving touch and weight, sensing who is leading and who is following the movement at any one time. We can pick up "felt messages" from each other. The following group of four exercises could easily slide into improvisation.

Massaging the back with the feet

An unusual form of massage with a partner. Take it in turns to be the active one.

Sit one behind the other. Then
Use the heels and balls of your
FEET to massage into your
Partner's back
Up and down the muscles on
Either side of the spine.

Ask your partner what feels
Good. If your partner leans back it
Increases the pressure.

Rub your feet alternately up and down
Try using every part of your foot.
Respond to each other. Then
Change roles.

Develop into movement improvisation using the feet and then other parts of
the body to press into and move a partner.

Feet meeting feet

With a partner
Try feet meeting feet —
Feet in contact — moving together — departing
Fascination with feet leading,
Feet moving your partner —
Touching and awakening other parts of the body
To encounter each other through the
Foot contact dance.

Head work

Good for slowing down a racing mind or alleviating a thick head.

Stand opposite your partner a foot away
Gently take your partner's head in your hands
And bring the top of your foreheads together
Slowly lean into that point of contact
So that you support each other's weight.
Flow into each other's forehead.

Keeping contact,
Gradually find ways of moving

Let your head roll along the surface
Of your partner's head. Do not hurry.

Support each other;
Two balls rolling together.
Let yourself go wherever the
Movement takes you.

Massaging the back with the head

Your partner can sit or lie down for this exercise.

Kneel behind your partner
Use your head to massage
Your partner's back.
Gently nudge and roll your head
Into all the soft parts.

This will feel good
To both of you.
Use it to loosen your own neck
And to sensitize your scalp.

Change roles and then try
Improvising together
Using your heads into
the backs of legs
the shoulders etc.

Often you will catch
Ideas from each other
And repeat them back.

Give and take

To prepare for this exercise, give each other's hands a gentle massage (see
'Self massage', pages 19–21).

> Stand facing your partner, placing your palms together.
> Lean inwards slightly, feeling connected through
> fingers, palms and heels of your hands.
> Feel your weight and sense the energy flow between you.
>
> Begin a gentle give and take action of pushing and receiving
> alternating hands, toward and away from your partner.
> Keep your legs soft and responsive to the movement.
> Enjoy the simple meditative quality of this partner contact.

Moulding your partner

This exercise suggests a lead and follow partner interplay. Partner A is moved
by the leading partner B, who through her touch, indicates movements . . .
lengthening, turning, rolling or sometimes supporting. The following partner A co-operates but tries not to anticipate the movement.

Partner A — choose a starting position, standing, sitting or lying.
Partner B — begin by focussing attention on your partner, getting a sense of
your partner's body; then decide which part of your partner you will touch/
move first.

> Gently change your partner's position
> And body shape
> Use any part of yourself —
> Your hands, head, knee . . .
> Stay sensitive to your partner
> At the same time be aware
> of the need to adapt your own body.
>
> Find a way to finish this exercise
> Then discuss it and change roles
> Try a different starting position.

How does it feel to be moved? How receptive are you to another's ideas?
How does it feel to lead your partner?
   A development of this is to change leaders at will.

Wheelbarrow style

In recreating childhood games we may rediscover forgotten strengths and skills; ways of being physically adventurous. Remember the wheelbarrow position? Hold your partner's legs while he walks on his hands.

> Help your partner
> Into the handstand position
> Find a satisfying way of
> Arriving there
> And proceed to hold your partner's legs
> While he walks on his hands.
>
> Then change roles
> It is a reminder of childhood
> Find out what it feels like
> Now.

"It was very strengthening to take my weight on my hands. It stretched out my back".

"It made me feel grounded to support your weight".

Swing the statue

In this gamelike exercise you can re-experience the excitement of feeling yourself fly through space, just over the edge of being in total control, trusting your reflexes to keep you safe. Make sure you try it outdoors or somewhere you have plenty of room. Perhaps do it slow motion first time through.

> Partner A holds Partner B's wrist
> with both hands and
> swings her round and round and round
> till she is running at arm's length.
> A releases her and lets her go flying.
>
> B holds the shape she lands in and
> not changing it at all, she moves in it,
> staying twisted and grotesque perhaps or
> huge and menacing, expressing
> the movement character.
> And then change roles.

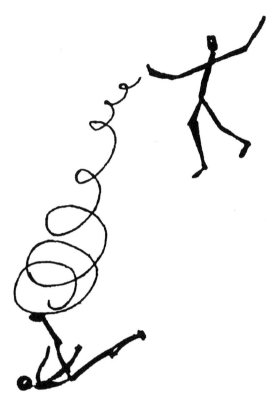

You can use this playform as a way of collecting starting point shapes which you return to later for an improvised duet.

Reflection on partner work

At the end of each encounter with a partner, there is the moment of separation, of no longer sharing the energy, of taking back full responsibility for yourself. This moment of separation is an important moment to acknowledge. It is also a profound experience which we face in daily life as we go from being together to being alone within various situations and relationships. Through movement we can abstract the event of separation and can focus on the feelings which arise.

SUMMARY — MAKING CONTACT

Any time you move together with another person whether you are touching physically or not, you are in a relationship with them. In this section, through

> – giving and taking weight
> – sharing energy
> – leading and following
> – using touch as a cue

you may experience elements of trust, sharing, cooperation and mutual support.

"...it is touch that gives us our sense of reality...our whole sense of what exists outside us is based upon the sense of touch."

Bertrand Russell
The ABC of Relativity

PART THREE

9

MOODS, MEMORIES AND DREAMS

In this section we explore moods, memories and dreams through movement. We stress the total involvement of our whole selves in this exploration: the physical, emotional and mental aspects of ourselves.

Often, our attention may be absorbed exclusively by what is happening physically, or by our thinking or by our emotional state. We do not give ourselves the time to integrate all three.

Here we focus on bringing them together as we explore embodying moods, memories and dreams. Through movement we can bring these inner contents alive in the present, finding the form which unites all the aspects of the experience. It is this dynamic integration which can give clarity and meaning to our expressive movement.

Movement as mirror

We may habitually hide our feelings, considering them to be inappropriate or excessive. As we cope with the external realities of our every day lives, the tendency is to give more importance to what we are doing than to what we are feeling. Doing can become divorced from feeling, and the expression of feelings can get left out.

We do not often answer the question, "Hello, how are you?" literally. The rejoinder is usually, "I'm fine." Because we have suppressed them for so long, we may be unaware of our feelings, unfamiliar with contacting and expressing them. This process may date right back to childhood when we naturally jumped up and down with excitement, stamped with anger or collapsed in tears, only to be disapproved of or punished. So, often we learnt to suppress our feelings together with an accompanying suppression in movement; for example, clenching the jaw muscles, tightening the stomach or bracing the knees. As adults many of our habitual movement responses now arise from these coping strategies we used as children.

Unexpressed feelings can be the source of muscular tension and pain. It is as if emotions become caught in our body, affecting both how we feel and what we look like. Our bodies, like mirrors, reflect our moods. As we gain more awareness of our habitual patterns, they may gradually begin to change.

We all need ways of expressing our feelings. Movement can offer an acceptable, satisfying and appropriate way of doing so. Although as adults we may communicate largely through language, movement offers a whole different mode of expression.

Feelings inexpressible in words find a way through in movement. Movement becomes symbolic of feeling and through it any intensity of feeling can be safely expressed.

Try using the energy of your feelings and transmute them into movement and dance. The medium of movement itself provides endless variety of expression. This experience is very different from venting your feelings destructively on your surroundings or other people. You are simultaneously expressing and shaping your experience while defining and developing the movement. This can be a very satisfying experience.

"There's a difference between saying how angry I am and moving my anger. Moving it certainly isn't the same as just talking about it".

"Sometimes I can't feel my feelings. I do not know what I feel. It's as if I am outside myself".

The middle of your body

> What do you feel in the middle of your body?
> Where is the middle for you?
> Put your hands there
> Focus there on the feeling tone
> Breathe into it
> Don't name the feeling
> Just let it penetrate into your consciousness
> And take you into movement if it will.

Open yourself to the idea of moving with whatever mood you feel.

The emotional breath

The dynamic quality of our breathing is directly related to our emotional life. Usually "holding our breath" or "not being able to get our breath" is connected to some sort of emotional holding, a holding back of expression. If we focus on the breath, particularly on gentle exhaling, we may feel more in contact with ourselves and our emotions and more able to express them in movement rather than locking them up, unresolved and painful, inside ourselves.

Move your mood

Use this exercise when you need an outlet for strong feelings or to help you recognize your feelings. Notice how the clearer you become in your movement the clearer you may be about your feelings, and how physical sensation and emotions are subtly connected. Find a quiet place to begin and choose a sitting, standing or lying starting position.

> First of all simply dwell on yourself
> Become aware of your body and how you feel in
> Particular parts of your body...
> Heavy, stiff, accelerated, tight?
> Do not try to do anything about it
> Breathe and focus on your body
> Give yourself plenty of time to become aware of your experience.

> Stay with the feelings however vague and then
> Gradually begin to take them
> Into movement.

> Movement may fluctuate in size, speed or shape
> Varying the rhythm.
> The feelings, or the movement may change.
> Images, associations and memories may
> Merge with the movement expression.

> Use all the parts of your body
> To articulate your feelings
> Give your feelings form.

Writing, drawing or talking are all ways of consolidating your movement experience. Working with a partner, communicating and sharing feelings and movement would be a further step.

"I noticed I felt depressed. My back felt tense. I started moving it gently. I imagine it warmed and comforted."

"I felt my shoulders pulling in and my jaw clenched. I increased that feeling and then my hands and arms went into strong movements."

An alternative way

An alternative way of working with movement and feelings is to begin with movement. Choose to move in contrasting ways and see what associations, particularly emotional associations, come up for you. For example, try

> Slow breathing stretches
> Quick articulations of the joints
> Very gentle rolling
> Strong gestures
> Different qualities of walking

Movement may well bring feelings to the surface. Each person's response to a given movement will be different. For example for one person the movement of rolling might be experienced as disorientating and frightening. To another it might feel challenging or joyful. Take plenty of time to become immersed in all facets of your chosen movement and its associations. Perhaps begin with some movement that feels familiar and safe. Be open to however the movement and feeling evolves. Then try a contrasting way of moving. You may want to collect some of your own movement ideas together and draw them into a dance.

It is the exploring of personal movement patterns and variations which create the individuality and excitement of each person's dance. There can be a continuous cycle of movement of feeling to form.

What moves you?

We can translate our inner thoughts and feelings into movement, thus making
them visible, giving them a form. In all movement work, the more awareness
there is of both feeling and form, the more meaningful it will be to ourselves
and to an observer.

When you observe movement, notice what moves you. Perhaps your
response is purely intuitive. The patterns of movement themselves convey
emotional significance.

Part of the performer's work in both dance and theatre, is to channel
the inner feeling into a clear outer form; and once the form is there, to keep
the feeling alive within it. In the symbolic language of movement, it is the
simultaneous fusion of feeling, movement and form which creates powerful
communication.

Physical patterns

Try noticing the habitual physical patterns in your own body and in others.
Try this at different times of day, in different situations ...

As you sit or stand, notice how you are in your body
Have a picture of yourself in your mind's eye
Could you literally draw it?
How would you describe yourself?

Are you perhaps
Hunching your shoulders
Holding your breath
Tightening your stomach
Pulling in your chin
Is your head tilted to one side
Are your toes curled under ... ?

Try intensifying what you observe
And then releasing it very gradually
Do this several times
Notice how you feel.

Additionally, try out the examples listed above whether or not they relate to
you. It's a way of getting into someone else's shoes.

Observing moods through movement

Through the observation of movement and posture we can notice the physical manifestations of feelings. In every day life we recognize a person's mood to be sad or angry or joyous before they even say a word. It is difficult to define exactly how we do this, but it is definitely something to do with the person's body and movement. Because movement communicates on an emotional level, we often, without analyzing, just know intuitively what it means.

Even before we recognize the face of a friend we see at a distance, we often know without a doubt that it is that person. Our personal movement style is as individual as our fingerprints, although it is difficult to interpret and define it in words. We all have certain movement preferences and physical patterns which are both learned and innate, and we can become aware of these.

"Movements reveal the thoughts and intentions of others more truly than do words."

Charles Darwin, 1872

Shadowing movement

> Watch the movement of others
> In the street, in a restaurant, on a bus . . .
> Focus on the non-verbal communication
> You receive intuitively from their movement.
> Observe them closely.
> Attune yourself to the physical sensations and
> Emotional feelings in your own body as you
> Empathise with another's movement.
> Try shadowing movement and see how it feels
> Explore interpreting movement behaviour.
> Does something about it touch a chord of
> Recognition in you?

It is not possible to say exactly and definitively what a movement means as there are many layers of meaning in movement. In addition our perception is always coloured by our mood, past experience, culture and values. But nevertheless, try translating your perception into words. What associations come to mind? Make the non-verbal verbal.

> *Empty can mean either*
> *Peaceful or desolate*

> . . .
> *Near the water there are skinless*
> *trees, fluid, greyed by weather*
> *in shapes of agony, or you could say*
> *grace or passion as easily*
> *In any case twisted.*

Extract from "Georgia Beach", from *Interlunar* by Margaret Atwood

Partner identification dance

Try on the movements of your partner.

> First of all
> How do you enjoy moving?
> How would you move
> Just as yourself?
> As you are now
> Dance out yourself
> And then take it in turns
> To copy each other
> Become the other person
> Through movement.
> When you dance as your partner
> Find out what forgotten parts of yourself
> You rediscover.

What special insights do you get from communicating in this way? Compare notes about what the movement meant to you both.

Movement metaphors

There are many familiar metaphors in which the description of the body is representative of a mood or feeling. The emotional connotation of movement is seen in:

> Keep your chin up
>   I felt weak in the knees
>   He elbowed his way in
>   I had butterflies in my stomach

It made my heart sing
It made my blood boil

She is a pain in the neck!

Continue the list of examples for yourself:
Then try spontaneously translating one of the metaphors into movement. Discover what sort of feeling arises when you do this. The results may
be unexpected and thought provoking. Perhaps discover new metaphors,
ones which have personal meaning for you.

Butterflies in stomach

Breathing sounds

Breath and sound go together from the beginning of our lives, with the wail
of the new born child. All vocal sound is produced in conjunction with an
inhale or exhale of breath. A different emotional quality can be felt in each.
Groans, shouts, sighs are usually expressed as we exhale. On an indrawn
breath we may gasp as in a moment of fear. We may hold our breath or become motionless.

Try playing with breath and sound
First become aware of your breathing . . .
Then play with breath sounds . . .
Gradually begin to vocalize your breath
Exploring all the different sounds
You can make on an inhale or an exhale
Sending them out from deep down in your centre.

Connect to the feelings that arise
And extend the sound naturally into movement.
Discover the variety of movement that arises
Through varying the pitch, pace and intensity
Take plenty of pauses...
As you express yourself through
Breath, sound, and movement.

Notice how the quality of the rhythm and emotions are intimately connected.

Face thoughts

Our thoughts and feelings are often reflected in our faces. We notice for example a smile, anxious eyes or pursed lips. We are quick to read the overt and underlying messages we receive from each others faces.

On the other hand faces can become like masks designed to cover up our true feelings. We may fear to expose our feelings or choose not to do so and thus try to keep our faces as neutral as possible. Interestingly we refer to "putting on a good face", one that does not express what we are feeling but is acceptable to other people.

We may be unaware of our habitual facial expressions. We often have unconscious tensions in our faces which are there constantly even as we sleep. Through the touch of our hands we can become more aware of these holding places, the tight jaw, the frown. Through gentle massage of the face we can begin to release them and may eventually release some of the inner conflict which they reflect.

(See 'Face massage', page 129).

Mask faces

Exercise your face and at the same time become aware of its expressive power. Try out each idea slowly, giving time for the rest of your face and body to join in with each facial expression.

Open your mouth wide
Screw up your face...
Widen your eyes...
Soften your jaw...

Lift your eyebrows
Narrow your eyes

> Clench your jaw
> Purse your lips
> Stick your tongue out
> Suck in your cheeks
>
> Find your own face moves
> Take your face
> Into your body.

Perhaps discover moods, characters and verbal connections.

Hand language

Our hands play a significant part in our emotional expression. Fear, anger, anguish, excitement or calm may all be manifested in the movement of our hands. Over time certain gestures have become ritualized and are immediately recognized for what they mean, for example, clapping, shaking a fist or bringing the palms of the hands together as in prayer.

> Begin to play with the emotional movement
> Of your hands, for example
> Gripping, pushing, Stroking, Shaking
> Take time to discover movements and their
> Personal significance to you.
> Feel them in your whole body
>
> Perhaps a sequence of these movements may
> Evolve for you like a story
> Each part having emotional associations
> And personal meanings
> Symbolized by the movement of your hands

As you explore this idea discover too the expressive significance of the *contact* of your hands on your body, for example fists on your hips, hands over your face.

Breathing into character

> Play with the rhythm of your breath
> Sighs ... gasps ... puffs ... yawns ...
> Once you get this breath-play going

Can you catch a glimpse of a character
Through the breathing
And start to consider your expression
In this way?
Let it naturally extend into expressive movement
Let yourself be totally involved.

Develop particular patterns of breathing and
Move as the character that emerges,
You may find that characters come and go
As your associations change from moment to moment.
From the timid one to the powerful
From the happy child to the grotesque witch.
Let your imagination flow with the
Drama of your breath.

When you reflect on this exercise, consider if the characters reflect some parts of yourself.

Walking into character

Try another exercise for unearthing characters from inside yourself. A particular way of walking may make you suddenly become old ... shy ... clumsy ... proud ... Discover what sort of characters you meet up with.

Walk around exploring the placement of weight on your feet.
Feel the difference between letting your weight fall
Through the heels ... balls ... inside ... outside ... of your feet.
Stay with each position long enough to

Let a specific character start to emerge.
Feel the effect filter through your whole body,
Changing its posture, its inner feeling, rhythm and pace.
Notice how even a subtle change of placement of weight
Changes everything!

Physical memories

Memories most often arise by way of thoughts and images, but there is a powerful physical aspect of memory too. The physical aspect and the associated emotional feelings of a memory can themselves be re-experienced. For example, we may have strong physical memories of a special place in nature or a time of dancing for joy or curling up close to a loved one.

By using physical memories in movement work we are in one sense reliving these experiences in the present. It is as if we bring our past feelings into the bloodstream of the present, so connecting the past to now. We often undervalue or cut off from our past feelings, but by reconnecting to them new awarenesses may emerge — we may feel more strongly rooted in present reality and perhaps more able to move forward into the future.

Our past is a valuable storehouse. We can all rummage around in the baggage of our past and find memories. Sights, smells, sounds, objects or tactile sensations experienced now, will often unexpectedly trigger a memory and things long forgotten will again be vividly present.

In exploring physical memories, approach the work with a spirit of adventure. You may tap into your unconscious and surprise yourself by recovering some bits of personal history which may be very pertinent to your life now.

Use the following exercises to explore this notion of physically remembering. Allow memories to bubble up from your unconscious so that you can feel them in your body now.

A today memory

> Remember a physical action or movement you made today.
> Just wait with your eyes closed. A memory will come.
> Notice how it makes your body feel,
> How it makes you feel.
> What associated thoughts and images arise?
> Dwell on the experience and take the essence into movement.

A past memory

> Close your eyes and allow memories from your past to arise.
> Visualize the scene...
> The space, the temperature, the smells, the sounds...
> Whatever stands out as important.
> Paint as complete a picture as you can.
> Focus on the movement aspects and
> Breathe them into the present.
> When the physical and emotional reality begins to recreate itself
> Let it move you where it will.
> Then rest in stillness with the memory/feeling for a while
> Before leaving it behind.

An earliest memory

> Let your mind drift all the way back
> As far as you can remember, and
> let a memory float up.
> Recreate the scene in your mind's eye.
> How old are you? Are you alone or are others there?
> Can you see them clearly? What are you wearing, and
> What parts of your body are you aware of?
> How are you feeling?
> Concentrating on this memory, let it affect your body
> See how you can explore the memory in movement.

Before babies have access to language, before there is an awareness of a world outside the Self, there is a physical awareness of sensations and feelings. These physical experiences, developed in us from birth or may be even before birth, form the basis of our earliest memories.

Louise Kaplan
Oneness and Separateness: From Infant to Individual

Memories from movement

Physical memories may be triggered by movement itself, perhaps taking you unexpectedly back to childhood.

The following responses arose from movement work:

"When you were swinging me, I had a memory of being held upside down. I felt disorientated, out of control".

"The movement reminded me of how my father used to spin me around holding one ankle and one wrist in a game we called airplane. I loved it".

"As I leapt down I remembered how I never attempted anything if I thought I might get hurt, and being cautioned that I might break a bone".

It is very clear that our early physical responses, even to the way we were handled as babies, affect our responses in later life.

A memorable object

Our possessions may also hold memories for us. Photographs, toys, books or clothing may have a particular significance and these can be starting points for movement. Choose a personal object or something that you feel drawn to in some way. Do not try to analyse why. Then sit or stand comfortably near it. Centre yourself to begin with by focusing on your breathing and your contact with the ground.

> Now just dwell on your chosen object
> for some time. Let any
> Thoughts, feelings and images
> Gradually emerge.
>
> Notice what is happening to your body
> For example is it softening, expanding
> Are small movements beginning?
> Begin to recognize your physical response
> And allow it to grow into
> Phrases of movement.
> Move away from and return to your object freely
> Use it in any way that occurs to you
> Welcome the unexpected.
>
> Sometimes be still
> And visualize your dance

Inside your head,
Imagine actions are like beads
On the thread of thoughts and feelings

Discover how past and present may merge
Make movement the bridge between
Then and. now.

In addition, objects which initially have no personal association may stir memories as we move in relationship to them, using their shape or quality. And equally, objects can be danced with from many other perspectives not necessarily related to memories.

Moving your dream

The Dream has poetry in it . . . layer upon layer of meaning, related to past, present, and future, and to inner and outer. And always fundamentally about oneself.

D. W. Winnicott
Playing and Reality

In working with your dreams, you may like to experiment with recording them, jotting them down when you wake up in the morning. Choose a dream to explore in the following exercise.

Lie quietly . . . breathe as if settling down to sleep . . .
Imagine the dream . . . Recall it as if
You are dreaming it now . . .
Then choose some aspect which stands out . . .
An image . . . a place, a person, an object,
Focus on your physical and emotional responses
Totally identify yourself with the image.
Become it.
Then let your body begin to move . . .
Without planning how, let it go into
Eyes-closed movement.

Gradually refine it by settling on a short, clear
Movement phrase . . . the essence of your exploration.
A metaphor for your feeling / image.

Choose other images from the dream, play other roles. Repeat the process. In dancing the dream you may gain insight into your unconscious. You may find that you change the dream and your response to it in the dance.

Dream themes

As we talk about our dreams we discover many themes that we all share, like

Journeys
"I travel the same route, but different things happen".
"I go to places I've never been before, usually in the South".
"I fly off cliffs, but I never arrive".
"When I fall it's terrifying. When I arrive it's okay".
"Just before I arrive, I change direction".

Rooms
" . . . new rooms in old houses".
" . . . broken houses I try to repair".
" . . . dark rooms appear again and again".
" . . . sunny rooms filled with animals".
" . . . it's hard to find the right room".

Time
"I have to wait. I must be patient".
"I'm in a hurry most of the time".

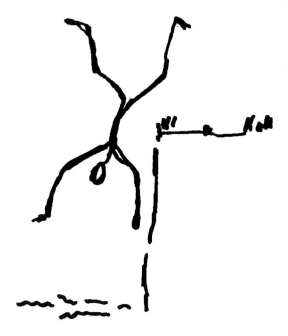

"I can never finish in time".

"It takes me a long time to get there. I'm moving in slow motion".

What are some of your dream themes?

Dream fragments

You do not need to recall a whole dream before choosing an idea as a starting point. You may be aware of a particular quality, action, mood or re-occuring image. Just a whiff of a memory can start you moving. It is as if you create your dream now. You may find that moving brings you into the feeling sense of dreaming. Movement may give you access to sudden flashes of dream memory unlocked from your unconscious. In this sense you will not be inter-preting a past dream but contacting again some of the issues and feelings which have arisen before in your dreams.

If you have the opportunity to work with others, you may all choose different starting points but then sometimes choose to interact and respond to each other's movement, so becoming for a while part of each others' dreams. Through this interaction and discussion of what arises you may share both movement and significant insights.

*By analyzing his dreams, a person can gain a much better understanding of himself
through comprehending aspects of his mental life which had escaped his notice, were
distorted or denied — not recognised before.*

Bruno Bettelheim
The Uses of Enchantment

SUMMARY — MOODS, MEMORIES AND DREAMS

In this section, we have explored how movement can be a way of form-
ing and expressing our inner world, making it visible to ourselves and
others.

We draw attention to the emotional aspect of movement, and how our
bodies are a source of

- feelings
- memories
- characters
- dreams

through which we may connect to, express, and integrate the various
aspects of ourselves.

*"Experiencing the present with the whole of my body instead of with the pin-
point of my intellect led to all sorts of new knowledge and contentment."*

Marion Milner
A Life of One's Own

10

LEARNING FROM NATURE

"There seems to be a universal need for silence, solitude, trees, sky, water, a reminder maybe of childhood and our complete identification with the physical world. Perhaps these inner landscapes of childhood are held within us and we try to recreate them."*

Many of us have lost contact with the actual **experience** of our connection to nature. Whether or not we are aware of it, our life rhythms are inevitably influenced by those of the natural world. Changes in the weather, seasons, phases of the moon, for example, do have a very real impact on our daily lives.

We need to keep an awareness of the tenuous balance involved in interacting with but not destroying our environment. Through movement we can develop a growing awareness of both self and surroundings and may hopefully become more responsible for the conservation of the natural world including ourselves.*

Stillness in a landscape

In stillness be open and receptive to the natural world. Feel the presence of the landscape around you. It is more than what you consciously see and hear. It is the sum total of all that the landscape contains and the impact of that upon your whole self.

> Being still in a landscape
> Gives you the time to
> Let your mind and body settle
> Time to take note of and to merge with your surroundings
> The landscape may offer soothing support and comfort
> Where you can let yourself just be
> Body opening, breath deepening

---

* From "Lost Connections" in *New Dance Magazine*. (R. S.)

Absorbing the atmosphere, the temperature, the view
The feeling of suspension from the "doing" of life
In this stillness you have the space
To feel what is really on your mind.

Contacting the landscape

Use the ground or natural objects in the environment to lie upon, lean against or hug, mould yourself onto...

Rest there in complete contact
Be aware of surfaces — soft, hard
Smooth, rough, warm or cold
Stay there, completely supported
Allow your body to receive sensations
Allow thoughts and images to surface.

After this waiting time
Slowly begin to respond in movement
To the tactile messages you receive
Stay in contact
Find what meaning is there for you
Discover aspects of yourself
That are special to this place.

"Lying down under the tree I listen to the sound of the leaves, smell that amazing, dry autumn smell. If I stayed here long enough I would be covered in leaves. The leaves know about falling and dying. There is wisdom here under this tree. It seems I can learn something from this place about listening, waiting and accepting..."

R. S.

Earth and sky breaths

From standing with the feet a little apart — a specific pattern of breathing and movement. Try it in Nature, or use your imagination in an indoor space.

> Stand with your arms relaxed at your sides
> As you breathe in draw your
> Fingertips up the front of your
> Body and stretch skywards.
>
> Then breathe out as your arms
> Open and your head hangs
> Forwards
> Relax your knees
> Hang downwards
> Exhaling through
> Your whole body
> Earthweighted.

Try developing the movement. Keep the rising and sinking but lead with different body parts.

Earth and sky breaths

Walking through

> Just walking across the earth is powerful.
> Feel the power of propelling yourself
> Adapting your movement to the given terrain.
> The pace ... the path ... the amount of space around.
> As you walk along
> Does the landscape suggest a style of moving through?
> The amount of energy required ... the feelings evoked
> The quality of restriction or freedom ... the view
> What does a particular landscape offer you?

Playing with a landscape

If you set out to interact playfully, what does an environment suggest?

> Sliding through sand, balancing on stones
> Skipping through fields, rolling down hills
> Hanging from trees, crunching through leaves,
> Do not have to be the
> Exclusive right of children.

> Let yourself breathe deeply
> Feel the childlike abandon of
> Responding with your whole self
> Enjoy the investigation
> Let yourself go and see what happens.

Establish a relationship with the environment by dancing, singing and resting within it. Feel yourself as part of it and discover your personal connections to its shapes, spaces, rhythms, textures and smells. We need to keep and cherish our essential connection to the earth.

Changing view

Slow down, look around, reflect on your surroundings, and then slowly begin to —

> Move in relationship to the distant horizon —
> To far away hills, clouds
> Or landscape vistas
> Respond in movement to the
> Feeling sense of endless space.

> Then in silence allow your gaze
> To scan from the horizon
> Back to the near view
> Of the landscape around you.

> Make contact with your immediate
> Physical surroundings.
> Watch yourself moving in
> Intimate relationship to —
> Stone, grass or hillside . . .

> Notice details, designs and rhythms
> In both your movement and the environment
> Enjoy your sensuous connection to nature.

Curt Sachs writes of a beautiful story about a dance told by the Orokaiva Papua people . . .

Once an old man sat gazing at the waters of a river when suddenly something lifelike appeared on the surface. A crocodile? No, it was a treetrunk which kept rising from the waves, then disappearing at definite intervals. The old man reached for his

drum and softly beat out the rhythm, and as he struck the drum, the picture of a new
dance took shape in his mind.

Curt Sachs *World History of Dance*

Body map

Lie down with eyes closed, and use this meditative exercise to make meta-
phoric connections between your body and nature.

> Imagine your body as a geographical terrain
> View it as you would a map
> Becoming familiar with the variety of territory.
>
> Take slow journeys down back roads
> Locating skeletal landmarks
> Hipbones, ribcage, collarbone, skull...
> The hills and valleys, the rough terrain,
> The unexplored regions
> Perhaps uncovering wells of deep feeling along the way.
>
> Your map is unique to you
> And like a geographical landscape is always
> Slightly shifting and changing.
> Moods, like changes in the weather,
> Create different tensions and energies
> Within your physical structure.

Get to know your body map like the back of your hand.

An imaginary landscape

Use this exercise as a starting point for improvisation. Accept whatever arises
— however fantastic the image.

> Close your eyes and allow the picture of a
> Landscape to form in your
> Mind's eye.
> Be there
> Breathe into it.
>
> Stay aware of yourself
> And your image.

Then gradually begin to move into your
Landscape, touching it with your body
Discovering movements and body shapes
As you travel through
Responding to your environment.

Play with movement and images
Bringing the imaginary landscape
Into your present surroundings,
Inside to outside.

Perhaps the imaginary landscape symbolizes aspects of yourself. Try writing or drawing your ideas too.

Landscape memories

Images from nature are often part of our memories or dreams. By recalling these memories of, for example, field, rock, tree or seascape, we can re-experience our responses to the natural world. Sometimes these memories may arise spontaneously into consciousness as we move, or we might deliberately choose one as a starting point for movement. Nature images may be powerful symbols of birth, growth and all our life processes.

*An image of a tree strongly rooted
With a huge spread of branches ...
Movement emerges from image
Movement and image intertwine*

*Rough texture of bark
Movement of feet and hands.
The smell of roots, the dark centre
Crouching and contracting, stretching,
Sun through fragile twigs
Walking
Leaf light*

Experiencing different aspects of tree and self...

R. S.

Happy places

Meditate on a happy place
Where you have been out of doors

Enjoying the natural surroundings
Where you have felt at peace with yourself
Dwell on what you
See, feel and hear
Enter again into
The colours, sights and smells
Of that place
Move in it if you wish
Know that in your mind
You can return to it
As a comfort, a refuge
An inspiration
Or a healing space
Like giving your mind
A holiday

"The sea is always here. I can always go back to it in my mind and refresh myself with it."

Water's edge

I am standing on the edge
Feeling soft foam caress my feet
Heels and toes and arches
Sighing with relief
Feeling themselves sink
In their own impressions

Toes splayed, disappearing into sand
Gripping strong like bird talons
If I stand here long enough
I will be embedded in the beach

I learn from the sand how I am supported
Through the bottoms of my feet

My toes come alive in the sand
They initiate a dance
Through my whole body

The urban landscape

The sense of vitality that we gain from nature we can also find through our
interaction with any environment.

Even on city streets
You can still respond to your surroundings
With a sense of aliveness and play
So that your going about isn't automatic
Keep a part of yourself the observer
Feel your subtle inner responses to the outer world
Energy, humour, frustration, excitement
The traffic, the crowds, the noise
Keep sensitive to the flow of movement
Make it all part of your ongoing dance
Down the stairway, under the bridge, up the escalator
The rhythm, the pace
Through the tunnel, around the corner
Stop, go, right, left
Watch the perspective change
Focus near, far, the overview, the details
Make choices, enjoy the journey
Within and without.

SUMMARY — LEARNING FROM NATURE

In this section, we have encouraged experiences which will reconnect us to the natural world of which we are a part. Through moving in relationship to landscape, we settle more deeply into ourselves,

recognizing – how our surroundings stimulate and motivate us
   – ourselves as a part of nature
   – real and imagined environments as sources of movement material

toward bringing about an intimate integration of self and nature.

"What I liked, and still like, is the way in which the panorama dominates me. The land is all view and I am all viewer, and soon the ecological patterns and colours not only spread before me but permeate me, and I become part of what I am seeing."

Ronald Blythe
Second Nature

11

THE EVERYDAY LIFE DANCE

In this final chapter we look at the "everyday life dance", and consider some practical ways in which we can reduce stress, revitalize ourselves and use our energy most effectively, to maintain a balanced rhythm between our inner and outer worlds.

In daily life the emphasis is usually on the outward aspect of our lives ... thinking, planning, doing, interacting. This is obviously necessary, but sometimes it can be to the detriment of our physical bodies and our sensory and emotional experience.

Even the most mundane aspects of life are part of the ebb and flow of energy, the currents and patterns of exertion and rest which make up the everyday life dance. We can learn to be attentive to these patterns in our lives, to recognize when we need to be active, when to pause, rest or reflect. Even in the smallest spaces of our day we can use simple exercises to help maintain the necessary balance between our inner world and the external demands made upon us.

" ... the sensory and emotional areas are left uncultivated to grow like weeds in a garden, rather than tended and nurtured for the full flowering of the human being"

Lee Strasburg *A Dream of Passion*

Everyday rhythm

As we become more aware of our bodies and ourselves, we may become more consciously aware of how we expend our energy, and notice our own particular rhythm of activity and rest.

We may discover our automatic patterns of behaviour are not to our best advantage. Some may find the pattern of "doing, doing, doing, doing ... collapsing" to be a familiar one. Sometimes we may push ourselves into activity when we need to rest, or 'go to sleep' when we would do better to activate ourselves. We are often not conscious of signals of imbalance until we are ill or in pain.

Through movement work we can become more aware of all the movement in our lives — our own movement, the movement of others, and the movement in the world around us. We can organize our lives according to various internal and external demands and decisions. We can move in harmony with the delight and fascination of our own everyday life dance.

Making spaces in the day

Find the small spaces in your day, and use them to nourish yourself.

> Before getting out of bed in the morning . . .
> Use the transition phase
> Between bed-warmth and rising
> Between dreaming and activity
> Allow this time
> Let it inform you
> About how you are feeling
> And what you need to do.
>
> At work
> Just for a few seconds
> Shift your attention
> Look out of the window
> Watch the clouds
> And take a breath . . .
> Then close your eyes
> And settle into your skin.

Keep a balance between giving out and taking in. Recognize the importance of not losing your sense of self. No matter how involving your activity may be, make spaces in the day for yourself. This space may be very short in duration. It is the quality of the time that is important. Focus on what you need to do . . . to meditate, take a breath or stretch, walk or run. Listen to your alternating need to be with others or alone. Aim to live in harmony with yourself, even if your rhythm is different from the world's around you.

Tunning in to tension

As you take more time for self awareness in your everyday life, your awareness of physical sensation may increase. You may literally feel more pleasurable as well as uncomfortable sensations, which may be experienced as feelings of tension or cold or stiffness.

Our natural response to discomfort is to try and somehow ignore it. Try allowing a bit of time in your day to listen to it. Sometimes by listening to discomfort, we can begin to alter it.

In stillness . . . imagine exactly what the discomfort looks like.
Let your mind go down to that place
To help define and warm it.
Focus your mind there.

Then, if you like, take it into small movements.
Let that develop as it will.
Explore what this means to you.

Tight body parts often represent inner conficts
Which we may be unaware of.
Bring them into the realm of thought and feeling by
Listening to them
Breathing into them
Giving them time and space.

What one sees clearly is usually a way of life that is passing.

Susan Griffin
Made From This Earth

Personal power and energy

There appears to be a clear relationship between movement and self empowerment. Movement literally increases physical and emotional expansiveness. After movement sessions people will often state that they feel more in touch with themselves, more connected and at one.

Whatever the size of the movement, by intimately connecting to it, we can experience its full intensity. In this way movement can empower us. We can become fuller through movement. We become simultaneously more of ourselves and more visible to others.

In our everyday life dance, when we feel this sense of personal power, we can use it like an inner source of energy to fuel our daily activity. We can enjoy the pleasure of feeling fully alive.

We can choose too to contain this energy and then to use it consciously as and how we will, rather than squandering it in unconscious action. This awareness of our energy level and how we are using our energy is vital to our wellbeing in our everyday lives

This awareness can also be a source of great power in performance work. For example:

A Fire Dance seen as part of a street theatre event. The dancer held flaming torches in each hand and moving very slowly made patterns of fire in the darkness. The dance grew gradually in intensity and range until his arms were whirling and circling around him and his whole body gyrated in the interweaving fire-light. It was an example of beautifully timed containment and release of energy and power.

Body image

How we feel about our body and the image we have of ourselves affects how we behave in the world. The subjective way we see ourselves can sometimes be a distortion as well as a distraction from really feeling ourselves.

A distorted body image can be formed from any number of internal and external pressures, like cultural standards of beauty and fashion, or family values and ideals. People commonly become fixated on a certain body part or parts which are not "acceptable". Often a negative body image is linked to a lack of self esteem.

The more we work with our bodies in movement, the more we can be really at home in our bodies. We have more possibility of both feeling ourselves and feeling good about ourselves.

Large and small spaces

Feel the effect on yourself of large and small spaces indoors and outside. For example.

" I feel hemmed in "

" There's too much open space for me "

" There's no room to manoeuvre "

Here our use of language reflects the connections we sometimes make between literal space and psychological space. Try the following exercise to reflect on your own responses to large and small spaces.

Move in a large space
or
A small space
Notice how you respond
In movement
Do you expand
or
Contract
What size movement
Feels comfortable
Here?
How does the space
Effect you?

Inhabit all the spaces of your Every Day Life.

Revitalize

Make use of your surroundings and objects around you to incorporate movement into your everyday life, to help stretch, strengthen and revitalize your
body. Do this anytime during your day. Use the stairs to strengthen and wake
up your legs, doorways to stretch your arms and shoulders. Be creative. Use
the furniture . . . a chair, a piano leg. Try lying on a soft rubber ball to contact
parts of you that feel stiff or sore and experience the gentle massaging effect.
Or lie with pillows under your knees to provide good support for your legs
to let go.

     Find exercises from the book which you can use easily during the
course of your daily life to release tension and stress.

     The following group of simple exercises are particularly suitable.

Squatting

Squatting helps to keep muscles and joints around the pelvis stretched and
active. Some people find it easy to stay in this position unsupported. With
regular practice squatting becomes easier. If you can do the exercise unsupported, aim for the armpits to be over the knees. You can also do this exercise
on your own by hanging away from the side of the bath or any solid object
which will support your weight.

(See also 'Counter balance' page 82)

Chair hang

As far as you can go . . .
For easing the back and improving the breathing

Sit straight on the chair
Knees opposite the hips
Feet apart under the knees

Slowly relax the head forward
Move forward from the hips
Past the knees
Exhale, let the weight go
So your upper body rests
On your knees
Arms and head dangling down
Breathe deeply. Feel the breath
In the lower back and the
Stretch along the spine

Slowly come upright again
Leave the head till last.

Towel massage for loosening the neck

Sit or stand
Take a thick towel loosely twisted
Hold it by both ends round the neck.

Let the head fall back
Supported by the towel
Slowly turn the head
From side to side
Feel the neck muscles
Loosen and relax.

Then with the head upright
Gently pull the towel
Back and forth
Its like drying the back of your neck
It feels good.

It's a towel massage for your neck.

Back to the wall

> Standing,
> Put your back against a wall.
> Feel it there behind you.
> With small movements, gently
> Rub and shift and nudge
> All the parts of your back, spine and
> Shoulders into the wall
> Find your sore spots.
> Enjoy the way the wall will
> Stay there. Use it for a
> Massage. Try up and down and
> Side to side, then keep in contact and
> s-l-i-d-e down to sitting.

Legs on the wall

After a hard day of walking, working, sitting, standing . . . try lying on your back and putting your legs up on the wall. It's a great position for resting and for feeling renewed circulation in your feet and legs.

> Lie close to the wall.
> Feel your back grow long and wide
> as you use the wall to support your legs.
> Feel how the bones seem to fall downward
> into the pelvis with the force of gravity.
>
> Walk your feet around
> using the muscles in your legs to press into the wall.
>
> Try letting your legs slowly open as wide as they can,
> stretching the muscles on the insides of your thighs.
> Rest in this position
> taking some nice deep breaths.
> Then, slowly, on the exhale
> bring your legs back together.
>
> Find your own movements
> Stretching, pushing, resting . . .
> through your foot and leg contact with the wall.

The orange squeeze

This exercise is useful for releasing tension in the body particularly in the
neck and shoulders. As you exaggerate and then release the tension notice
any difference in your feelings.

> From sitting or standing lift your shoulders up and back
> and your head back and down
> Imagine squeezing a tiny orange on the back of your neck
> Feel the base of your skull press your shoulder muscles
> Squeeze and then exhale and let your head relax forwards.
>
> If you enjoy the squeezing sensation
> Take it into other parts of your body
> Any part of you that feels tight
> And needs releasing
> Squeeze away those tight, protective, anxious
> Parts and allow in other moods.

Face massage

During the massage exhale through your mouth with gentle hissing or blowing to help release the lips and jaw muscles.

> Gently cover your face with your hands
> Let your jaw relax
> Feel the light touch of your fingertips
> On eyelids and forehead
> Give your face the healing touch of your hands.
> Allow your hands the comfort of holding your face.
>
> Then use the flats of your fingers
> To massage your face firmly
> Moving the skin in small circles
> From the centre of the face
> Outwards and upwards.
> Relax your jaw. Feel your skin
> Loosen and soften
> Over the bones like a
> Mask melting.
>
> To finish, cup your jaw between your palms.
> Slowly and lightly slide your hands
> Up over your cheeks, forehead and scalp
> Into your hair and off your head
> Clearing yourself of unwanted thoughts.

Brushing cares away

Connect long sighing exhales to each phrase of this exercise.

> Rest the fingertips of both hands on your forehead
> And lightly stroke over the top of your head
> Down the back of your neck, round the collar bone
> And then
> Down the front of the body, legs and off your feet.
>
> Again from standing reach across yourself
> And brush down from the centre of your neck
> Over your shoulder and down each arm in turn.
>
> Then reach up behind you and stroke down your back
> Back of your legs and off your heels.

Stay in that hanging down forwards position
Release a long sigh and
Let tension pour away into the ground.

Lying down

Lying down can help us to be more aware of our bodies. We literally *feel* ourselves more when more of our body is in contact with the ground. Once as
babies we supported ourselves in many different ways; on our backs, sides,
stomachs or hands and knees. This close, physical contact with the ground
helped us to discover and explore ourselves. Now as adults we tend to spend
most of our time upright on our feet rarely contacting the ground more ex-
cept when lying down to sleep.

Lying down need not only be a prelude to sleep but a time which is
conducive to relaxation and thought. Lying down can be a positive and creative experience, allowing one to feel an inner stillness and awareness of self.
As we let our eyes and thoughts wander we may "dream awake" and have
insights which perhaps would not occur to us in the more objective state of
the upright position.

Make some lying down spaces in your day. Re-experience your tactile
relationship with the ground.

*"When you suggested that I lie on my back with my knees up, I was delighted. Four
times a day? That's just what I feel like doing!"*

Grounding

When we are grounded we are aware of our physical connection to the earth.
When we lose the felt sense of ourselves, this usually implies a lack of contact
with the ground. It is this groundedness which helps us to feel substantial
and affirms our own reality. Take time to really feel your contact with the
ground.

(Refer to the exercises in Parts 1 and 2 which help in grounding yourself.)

The essential self

Who am I in this
World behind my skin

Into my bones into the
Very depth of me.

I am what I feel
What I imagine
And what I see
But I am also
Indefinably more than
All of this.

R. S.

Aside from our roles, our work, our relationships, we may discover our essential selves, the unique core attributable to each of us. We need to respect and value this individuality in a world which increasingly undervalues it.

SUMMARY — EVERY DAY LIFE DANCE

In this section we become more aware of how we balance the movement and rhythm of our lives, and what we need to sustain us. We focus on practical ideas to nourish and support us to move in harmony with the dance of our every day life

through exploring
- how we use our bodies in daily life
- our relationship to the spaces we encounter
- our balance between activity and rest
- the experience of tension and pain.

In so doing we may support our movement toward health and growth.

BIBLIOGRAPHY

Atwood, Margaret, *Interlunar*, London: Cape, 1988.

Bettelheim, Bruno, *The Uses of Enchantment*, London: Thames and Hudson, 1976.

Blythe, Ronald, *Second Nature*, London: Cape, 1984.

Chekov, Michael, *To the Actor*, NY: Harper and Row, 1953.

Eliot, T. S., *The Four Quartets*, London: Faber, 1959.

Gibran, Kahlil, *The Prophet*, London: Heinemann Ltd., 1926.

Griffin, Susan, *Made From This Earth*, London: Women's Press, 1982.

Jodjana, Raden Ayou, *A Book of Self Re-Education*, London: L. N. Fowler, 1981.

Kaplan, Louise, *Oneness and Separateness*, London: Cape, 1979.

Larsen, Stephen, *Shaman's Doorway*, NY: Harper and Row, 1976.

Milner, Marion, *A Life of One's Own*, London: Virago, 1986 (1934).

   On Not Being Able to Paint, London: Heinemann Educational, 1950.

Paz, Octavio, *The Labyrinth of Solitude*, London: Penguin, 1961.

Rogers, Carl, *On Becoming A Person*, London: Constable, 1967.

Russell, Bertrand, *The ABC of Relativity*, London: Unwin Paperback, 1985.

Sachs, Curt, *World History of Dance*, NY: W.W. Norton & Co., Inc., 1963.

Strasburg, Lee, *A Dream of Passion*, London: Bloomsbury, 1988.

Tulku, Tarthang, *Gesture of Balance*, Berkeley, Ca: Dharma Publishing, 1977.

Watson, Lyall, *Gifts of Unknown Things*, London: Hodder and Stoughton, 1976.

Winnicott, D. W., *Playing and Reality*, London: Tavistock Publications, 1971.

INDEX

passim refers to words mentioned frequently throughout the book

skin, 63
spine, 35, 37, 40, 45, 46
space, *passim*
stillness, *passim*
Strasburg, L., 121

Tulku, T., 18

visualization, *passim*

Watson, L, 16
Wigman, M. 42
Winnicott, D. W., 107